BARKER

A GUIDE ❧ IN WORD AND PICTURE ❧

TO THE FABULOUS GOLD CAMP ❧ OF

THE CARIBOO ❧❧❧ BY BRUCE RAMSEY

PRINTED IN CANADA

First Printing: December 1961
Second Printing: May 1966

MITCHELL PRESS ❧ VANCOUVER ❧ CANADA

CONTENTS

	Page
THE MINES	1
LIFE IN BARKERVILLE	23
THE LAW	51
THE FIRE DEPARTMENT	55
CHINATOWN	59
BARKERVILLE'S CHURCHES	62
BOWRON HOUSE	65
THE CEMETERY	67
THE ROAD IN	85

INTRODUCTION

IN THE DAYS when the province of British Columbia was young, Barkerville was one of the most important names on the map north of San Francisco. Along its muddy, uneven single street and back alleys strode men and women representing all types of humanity: miners, both inexperienced and experienced; doctors, nurses, parsons, judges, tamed-down gunslingers, faro bankers, dance hall girls, tinkers, tailors, soldiers, sailors, rich men, poor men, beggar men and thieves.

It has been said that Barkerville is a ghost town; perhaps it is, and perhaps it isn't. It all depends on what is implied by the term "ghost town." If it means "abandoned," then Barkerville isn't, and never has been, a ghost town, but if the phrase is used in the sense that the past haunts you, that its past is everywhere you look, then this rustic town, resting in the valley of Williams Creek, is, without a doubt, a ghost town.

The purpose of this little book is to bring to the visitor an explanation of the "invisible" Barkerville, which draws thousands of visitors each year, instilling in them, for want of a better word, "something"—for who can describe this feeling as anything else but "something"—which cannot be shaken off or soon forgotten. The visible Barkerville, without the memories, would be like a cake without icing, or a car without a motor.

This, then, is Barkerville, the "gold capital of British Columbia."

Billy Barker

THE MINES

THE GOLD EXCITEMENT began at lunchtime on March 23rd 1858, and it hasn't really stopped since. For several years before that, alert men, ever susceptible to even a whisper of that magic word "gold," had been hearing enticing rumours that the precious yellow metal was being taken from the creeks in British territory somewhere north of the 49th parallel. The country was vaguely known by a handful of fur-traders, who were not anxious to encourage the stories, and maps were practically non-existent. The country went under the general heading of "New Caledonia," a name given to it by Simon Fraser of the North West Company in 1808, but to the servants of the Hudson's Bay Company, the successors to the N.W.Co., it had a far more sinister name—"the Siberia of the fur trade"—on account of its remoteness from civilization, that is, the Atlantic seaboard, and in particular, Montreal.

But on this spring day of 1858, the key was turned to unlock the doors and begin the opening up to settlement of what is now the province of British Columbia. A party of miners, bound for the Thompson River country where gold was reported, stopped to have lunch just below Fort Yale, near the point where the mighty Fraser River spews out of the formidable canyon. Almost without looking for it, the men found rich ground, and the spot became known as Hills Bar, "the first worked, the richest and the longest worked bar" on the Fraser.

From that moment the fur trade which had been the sole industry of the country was doomed, for fur and gold do not go together.

Word soon reached San Francisco, which because of the collapse of the mining boom in California sorely needed a shot-in-the-arm, and the news raced from saloon to saloon, from house to house, until the city by the Golden Gate was caught up in an epidemic of gold fever the like of which not even it had known before. Every conceivable type of craft was commandeered for the voyage north to the new El Dorado. Some of the ships were not much more than hulks, but at least they floated, or there was a pretty good chance that they would remain afloat long enough to get them to "Frazer's River."

"The whole of California in April 1858 was in a ferment," wrote Hubert Howe Bancroft, the noted historian. "Business in the interior was deranged, and in many places broken up. Hundreds too impatient to wait for the steamers mounted horses and hastened overland. . . . [It was] estimated that in May, June and July, 23,000 persons went from San Francisco by sea and about 8,000 overland. . . ."

However, the Fraser played nasty tricks with the miners, for just as they arrived she went into flood, hiding the gold, at least temporarily, until the waters receded later in the year. By the time that happened, many had returned to San Francisco saying "Frazer's River" was a

Edward "Ned" Stout

"humbug." Some of those who stayed were caught in the treacherous currents and were dashed to pieces on the jagged rocks of the canyon, but the river was fighting a losing battle.

After Hills Bar came a host of others, ranging from Fargo Bar, near Sumas on the lower Fraser, right up to Pavilion, and up the Thompson to a point about 15 miles north of the mouth of the Nicola River.

During July and August, recoveries of bodies of white men floating down the river were common at Yale. There was a state of terror in the canyon. The cause of the trouble, it is said, was a combination of influences: the desire of the Indians to monopolize the mining, coupled with the success of the Indian wars then raging in Washington, plus the arrogance of the miners who lived by the code that the only good Indian was a dead one.

Caught up in this Indian warfare was one Edward "Ned" Stout, one of the men who was to play a key role later on in the Barkerville story.

Stout, with 20 others, was working his way up the canyon towards the Thompson when they were attacked by Indians between Hell's Gate and Boston Bar. All day long they battled the enemy, and, as night fell, the besieged men moved quietly about constructing a rude form of fortification at China Bar. Soon after sunrise they were greeted by a shower of arrows and bullets. The attack lasted all day, and one by one the miners were picked off. By luck, another party of miners, bent on making peace with the canyon Indians, arrived—and just in time, too.

The party had been reduced to five and all the survivors were badly wounded.

Following this narrow escape, Stout worked his way up the Fraser towards Lillooet, then to Fort Alexandria and on to the mouth of the Quesnel River, following it to the Forks, where already a few men were at work.

From this point, and the little town of Quesnelle Forks which grew as a result, Antler Creek and Cedar Creek were found to be good placer streams, and more and more miners began to arrive. One of these was William "Dutch Bill" Dietz, who had come up from the California gold-fields where his luck hadn't been too good. Dietz, too, had trouble with the Indians. Near Lillooet a band of natives had stolen all his supplies, forcing a return to Yale, but in the spring of 1860 he started out again, slowly and arduously working his way northward.

The snow still lay deep on the ground, and perhaps it wasn't the best time for mining, but Dietz was impatient, and so early in February 1861 he started out from the Forks, up towards Keithley Creek, and over the divide. With him were two companions, and one night they camped beside a small stream which they named William Creek, in honour of their leader, "Dutch Bill."

The Victoria *Chronicle* for November 5, 1863, told the story of what was to be one of the greatest gold discoveries in the world:

"On the following morning they eagerly commenced to prospect. They found prospects on the north-west side of the creek varying from ten to thirty cents to the pan near the bedrock. After that one of the party sunk another hole on the east side . . . and obtained a similar result. Night coming on, and much time having been lost through having but one pick (the other having been left at Antler Creek because they thought that shovels would be more required for stripping off the snow), they abandoned their work for that day and lit a fire to cook supper. But Dutch William, restless and enterprising, left the others basking before the burning logs, and traveled up the creek until he found the bare bedrock cropping up in the stream. . . . He tried one panful of gravel, but obtained none of the precious metal. He tried another taken from the side near where there was a high ledge, and to his great delight found himself rewarded with a dollar to the pan. The gravel was frozen hard to the rock and when detached with difficulty thawed in the cold stream. Time passed quickly, and he was soon obliged by darkness to return to his camp fire. He showed his companions the prize he had obtained, but they possibly hardly believed his statement, for they determined to return to the Forks. He, having no pick, was obliged, unwillingly, to return with them, though he had provisions for some days more. On reaching Antler he obtained the co-operation of John Metz and two others, and the party, now numbering four, all returned to William Creek by a shorter road. . . . Two went into the cañon to prospect, and two began in the ground above;

the former got a dollar to the pan in five feet of gravel, but those who worked in the higher ground failed to obtain gold in paying quantities. After being out seven or eight days . . . three started for Antler for provisions, one remaining to protect the claims taken up by Metz and William for their respective partners. Before making the secret known they had intended instituting a more thorough examination of the creek, that the discoverers might have the choice of ground. William, however, found that his secret had been guessed soon after his arrival at Antler, and, leaving his companions to bring up the stores, he started back at daybreak for his new creek, making the distance, on show shoes, in the wonderfully short time of three hours over an unblazed trail. But his strenuous exertions were unavailing; the whole population of Antler had tracked his steps, and within two or three hours of his arrival, the whole creek was staked off into claims over ground covered with eight feet of snow. He next packed a rocker from Antler, upon his back, and blazed the trail with a hatchet, that persons passing might avoid the danger which occurred from men daily being lost for hours. Keeping two of his partners at work at Keithley, to provide the others with means, he determined to put a flume in the cañon, which was the only claim he had secured. Money and provisions being scarce, this determined man with his mate sawed lumber from four in the morning until eight at night, and put up the first flume on the creek, 170 feet long, four feet wide and two feet deep. But when they obtained pay for their labor, they found that instead of fifty dollars they could only get twenty dollars per diem."

When that story appeared in the *Chronicle,* Dutch Bill Dietz was in Victoria stone broke, and suffering great pain from a sickness developed in the Cariboo.

Williams Creek at Richfield

"He has succeeded in doing much for his country and in pointing out the road to fortune for many, but he has made no competency for himself," said the newspaper.

Dutch Bill never hit pay dirt again, and in 1877 he died in poverty.

Around these diggings grew the town of Richfield, a name given to it by Lieutenant H. S. Palmer of the Royal Engineers who surveyed it. For a time it was known unofficially as Elwyntown, in honour of Thomas Elwyn, gold commissioner for the Cariboo, but this name, honourable as it was, did not in any way convey the richness of the placer fields at its front door. While the other towns which later sprang up further down Williams Creek could boast of being bigger, brassier and wealthier, none could lay claim to having a court house. At first the courts were held in a log cabin, but this soon proved inadequate, and the present building was erected on the site of the old. Today this building is the sole remaining vestige of Richfield's past, and continued to hold some importance until about 1914 when the Court House at Quesnel was opened.

From Williams Creek, the miners branched out, and virtually all the streams within a 20-mile area were found to be gold-bearing. In July, 1861, Ned Campbell struck it on Lightning Creek, and in 1862, Richard Willoughby, an experienced frontierman, found the Lowhee, which he named after a secret society formed by the miners in 1858 at Yale.

Richfield Court House

William Cunningham, after whom Cunningham Creek was named, wrote a most extraordinary letter to "Dear Joe" from Williams Creek, on May 18, 1862. Gordon Elliott in his *Quesnel, Commercial Centre of the Cariboo Gold Rush* quotes it:

> Dear Joe.
>
> I am well, and so are all the rest of the boys. I avail myself of the present opportunity to write you a half dozen lines to let you know that I am well, and doing well—making from two to three thousand dollars a day! Times good—grub high—whiskey bad—money plenty.
>
> Yours truly,
>
> Wm. Cunningham.

As its name implies, Richfield was rich, and when reports of the strikes reached Victoria they were followed by the appearance of ragged miners,

Government Buildings at Richfield

staggering under the weight of the gold they carried. Naturally, with this evidence at hand, a rush ensued, and with the miner came the saloon-keeper, the faro banker and others, just as intent on relieving the miner of his gold as the miner was to relieve the creek of its precious yellow content.

Below Richfield, in the canyon of Williams Creek, the gold suddenly gave out, and nobody could figure out why until nearly 30 years had passed.

One of the first to venture below the canyon was the old Indian fighter Ned Stout, and at the mouth of the gulch which now bears his name he found his gold. Just about this same time, an ex-sailor by the name of Billy Barker, who had jumped ship on hearing of the Fraser River excitement, arrived in Richfield.

Moving down the canyon, and past Stout's claim, he selected a spot

6

Canyon of Williams Creek

back from the river a bit, and at 52 feet, on August 21, 1862, found the richest paydirt anybody had ever seen. With his pockets full of gold, Billy Barker bounded for the first saloon he could find—and they weren't hard to locate, either.

Bishop George Hills, the Anglican prelate from Victoria, noted in his diary these terse words:

"When lead struck on Barker's claim about August 21st, all went on a spree for several days, excepting one Englishman, well brought up."

This Englishman was not Billy, for he was having the time of his life, and above the roar of the miners, and the tinkling of bottles on the bar his voice could be heard singing out his little ditty:

> I'm English Bill,
> Never worked, an' never will.
> Get away girls,
> Or I'll tousle your curls.

Billy's discovery immediately swept away the "humbug" stigma with which Williams Creek had been associated. At Richfield, the diggings were shallow, and gold could be secured by diverting the stream through a length of sluice boxes, but below, where Barker had made his strike, the gold lay deep. This was the luck, and the curse, of Williams Creek,

7

for it took capital to sink the shafts, and capital to erect the great water wheels—similar to that on display in Quesnel—to keep the shafts clear of water.

With Billy Barker in this fabulous claim were six other Englishmen, and around their building, a rough, log-walled shafthouse, grew the town of Barkerville, at first known as Richfield Lower Town. It was just like Topsy: it grew and it grew. The first businessman to appear on the scene was a Mr. William Winnard, who was to remain in Barkerville for many years as a blacksmith. Within a year, Barkerville boasted a floating population of 10,000 persons.

Unofficial records credit Barker's claim with a production of $600,000, but Bill's share did not last him long. During the winter of 1862-63 he went "outside" to Victoria, and there married a London widow by the name of Elizabeth Collyer, whom he brought back to the Cariboo with him.

This was a big mistake, for with hundreds of younger men about (Barker was 42 and slightly bow-legged) and few other women, he found he had to step pretty lively—and spend pretty lavishly—to keep his place in his wife's affections. Billy began to drink even harder than usual, and pretty soon the saloon keepers, of whom there were many, had all Barker's money. And with Billy broke, Elizabeth went on her way.

Although a good percentage of his gold was pushed over the polished mahogany of the saloon, he nevertheless was generous in grubstaking other prospectors.

The Barker Claim

The Barker Claim today

Billy had struck it rich once, and he felt sure he could do it again. But he couldn't. Luck was against him. People up and down the creek owed him money which he couldn't collect. Finally, in desperation, he took a job as cook on the government road, but his troubles were not over; a sore appeared on his lower lip which refused to heal, and on July 11, 1894, a broken man, Billy Barker died of cancer in the Old Man's Home in Victoria. His obituary in the newspapers was only about 200 words in length and it included a lecture on the folly of not saving anything for his declining years.

Billy Barker's Watch and gold pouch, prized possessions of the Barkerville Museum

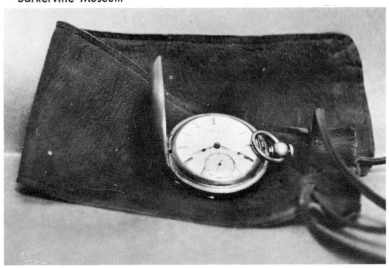

About a mile from the Barker shaft, John A. "Cariboo" Cameron was making his niche in the golden history of the Cariboo.

John and his wife Sophia, who hailed from Cornwall in what is now Ontario, landed in Victoria in March, 1862, and in August the pair staked their claim, but Sophia never lived to see how successful this rugged plot of ground would turn out to be, for on October 22, 1862, she died of mountain fever.

Cameron worked feverishly, and on December 2, 1862, while snow lay deep around, a shovel full of dirt revealed more gold than he had ever dreamed of owning. And he was determined that the gold would be made to pay respect to his wife's memory.

Although she had been buried a couple of days after her death, Cameron had the body disinterred, and offered $12 a day and a bonus of $2,000 in gold to anyone who would help him take the coffin from this womanless land to Victoria. Up to the very last minute, no one volunteered, but finally Robert Stevenson, Cameron's partner, offered to go "but not for gold." The 400-mile trip in 40-below weather took 36 days to complete. The second "provisional" funeral was held in Victoria on March 3, 1863, with Cameron and Stevenson the only mourners at the graveside. She

Wedding picture of John and Sophia Cameron (centre)

Cameron Claim

remained there until November 7, 1863, when a ship took her remains to Panama, and from there they were despatched to Cornwall, arriving about Christmas time. But even there, she could not rest in peace. It was rumoured that Sophia was not in her coffin, and that instead, it was filled with gold. Again the body was disinterred to prove, once and for all, that the stories were untrue, and then Sophia was left in peace.

Cameron now decided to settle near Cornwall, and purchased a 200-acre farm near Summertown. He spent vast sums of money modernizing it, and invested in many enterprises, none of which was successful, and soon he was as broke as when he first arrived in the Cariboo.

Broken in spirit, he returned to Williams Creek to try and wrest a second fortune, but the Cariboo had changed. It was no longer the place for the single miner; the era of mechanical mining had arrived, and to a miner without a purse, it was hopeless. Fifteen years to the day on which his Sophia's body left Victoria, Cariboo Cameron died, on November 7, 1888, and his friends buried the unhappy pauper in the little graveyard which he had himself selected for one of his workmen killed on the Cameron claim.

Around Cameron's claim, just like Barker's, there grew a town and it soon had its saloons, hotels and restaurants, and a library.

A correspondent to *The Province*, then a weekly published in Victoria, signing himself "Cariboo", has left us a description of the naming of this

CAMERONTON

A Town with hotels and Saloons once occupied these benches near "Cameron's claim". The famous 'diggings' were staked on Aug. 22nd 1862, with 7 persons originally holding ground and making a total claim of 300' X 700'. Gold was struck 40' down in Dec. 1862 and by next Oct. "Cariboo" Cameron had made $350,000.00

town, which, incidentally, was named before Barkerville. It appeared in the issue of November 9, 1895:

"A christening I need scarcely say was a rare ceremony in Cariboo in the early days. There were no children . . . but we had a christening without a child. The ceremony was performed by the late Rev. Mr. [Ephraim] Evans one bright Sunday in August 1864, in the presence of a large and distinguished crowd. And as if to insure that everything was done according to law the late Sir Matthew Baillie Begbie, Judge Cox and Judge Reilly [Peter O'Reilly] were present. All the miners of the district gathered around, and with due solemnity the parson named Cameronton in deference to the wishes of the people. . . . There was a prayer, the singing of a hymn or two and a nice little sermon. Service over we proceeded to drink the health of Cameronton. If the liberality and enthusiasm displayed on that occasion could have made the place anything like what we wished for, Cameronton would long since have been the most populous and prosperous city in the province.

"Oh, what a time we had! The following morning some of the boys were looking for a shoehorn to put their caps on."

From all parts of the world, men arrived to harvest the gold, and the harvest was truly bountiful. Writing years later, Dr. George M. Dawson,

Grave of Cariboo Cameron, Barkerville

the distinguished Canadian geologist and one-time director of the Geological Survey of Canada, had this to say:

"Williams Creek has yielded more gold than any other creek in British Columbia. As examples of its yield in early years, Steele's claim gave a maximum yield of 409 oz. or $6,544 a day. More than $100,000 in all was taken from this claim of 80 feet by 25 feet. In 1862 Cunningham's claim produced gold to the value of nearly $2,000 a day for the season, while on several days as much as 52 lb. weight of gold was taken out. The Adams claim yielded to each of its three partners $40,000 clear. These claims were above the canyon in shallow ground. The deep ground below the canyon was first bottomed toward the end of 1861 by the Barker Company. . . . The Diller Company was the next most successful to this, and it is credibly stated that here, on one occasion, 200 lb. of gold worth $38,000 was obtained in one day. In 1863, three claims below the canyon yielded $300,000 and 20 claims were steadily producing from 70 to 400 oz. a day."

Diller had always dreamed of mining his weight in gold and as the record above states, he did much better than that. He returned to Pennsylvania, and made a second fortune in the U.S. civil war.

The Caledonian claim, seen as you drive into Barkerville, yielded at one time from $5,000 to $6,000 per day. The Raby, nearly opposite

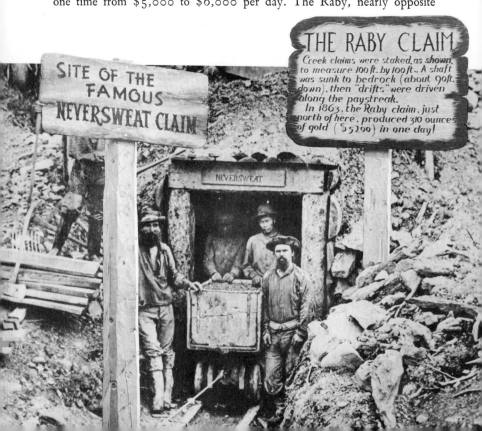

SITE OF THE
FAMOUS
NEVERSWEAT CLAIM

THE RABY CLAIM

Creek claims were staked, as shown, to measure 100 ft. by 100 ft.. A shaft was sunk to bedrock (about 90 ft. down), then "drifts" were driven along the paystreak.

In 1863, the Raby claim, just north of here, produced 310 ounces of gold ($5200) in one day!

NEVERSWEAT

One of Frank Laumeister's camels—Grizzly Morris's "bear"

the Cameron, produced 300 ounces in a day's washing, and from the Neversweat $100,000 was taken out of a 120-foot claim. Another star in the galaxy of mines in the proximity of the Cameron was the Grizzly, which adjoined the present-day Paintbrush Picnic site. It was named after "Grizzly" Morris, one of eight who originally staked the claim. The year before it was sold by the sheriff, Morris was offered $7,000 in cash for his interest in it. When the claim was in full swing, the weekly paysheet was not less than $10,000.

Grizzly Morris has the distinction of bagging the most fantastic "grizzly bear" on record. One day, a couple of years before making his strike on Williams Creek, he was near Beaver Lake on the road "in" to Quesnelle Forks, and peering through the bush he saw the largest grizzly he had ever seen in his life. Taking aim, he fired, and the animal toppled over. And what a bear it was! It was one of Frank Laumeister's camels!

In October 1863, Barkerville greeted its first "tourists", the Viscount √ Milton and his companion, Dr. W. B. Cheadle, who had crossed the prairies and the Rockies, not in search of gold, but just to see what was going on. Cheadle wrote in his diary that en route they met "a small bullock wagon escorted by about 20 men on foot. This proved to contain 630 pounds weight of gold, the profits of a Mr. Cameron, the principal shareholder in the noted Cameron claim. This gold, worth about £30,000 had been amassed in the short space of three months and represents probably less than one-half of the actual production of the mine during that time."

They also watched the "clean-up" at the Raby claim, where 310 ounces were taken out. The Ericsson, which opened in 1863 yielded a weekly average of 1,400 ounces. Of this mine, James Douglas, governor of British Columbia recorded that in 1864 the claim paid $8,000 to the share, or a total of $90,000 clear of expenses, and in 1865 the dividends were $14,000 to the share.

Milton's and Cheadle's diary and subsequent book, *Northwest Passage by Land*, is filled with interesting tid-bits of information and anecdotes. They tell of a Cariboo man who, having made $30,000 to $40,000 during the season of 1862, went down to Victoria to enjoy himself. At a saloon he treated all he could find to all the champagne he could make them drink. The champagne held out the longest, all of the company gathered from within and without being unable to consume the bartenders' stock. Our man then ordered every glass remaining in the establishment to be filled, and with one grand sweep of his cane, sent them spinning off the counter. Still the champagne held out. To win his victory over the last hamper, he jumped upon it, cutting his shins. Having still a handful of gold pieces with him, he walked up to a large mirror worth several hundred dollars adorning one end of the room and, to prove that gold was sovereign of all things, he dashed a shower of his heavy pieces into the face of his own image, shivering it to fragments. The next year he was working as a labourer.

By the end of 1864 the happy-go-lucky era had ended; the shallow diggings up near Richfield had been worked out and the cost of working the deeper claims, below the canyon, had discouraged many who returned to the "outside" or got employment with the larger mining companies.

This was monotonous work—in comparison with the thrill of anticipation in finding your own gold—and James Anderson, the poet-laureate of the Cariboo, caught this feeling of drudgery in a poem he wrote for the *Cariboo Sentinel*, Barkerville's little newspaper. It's called *Song of the Mine* and was written May 1, 1869.

> Drift! Drift! Drift!
> From early morn till night.
> Drift Drift! Drift!
> From twilight till broad daylight,
> With pick, and crow-bar and sledge,
> Breaking a hard gravel face;
> In slum, and water and mud.
> Working with face-board and brace;
> Main set, false set, and main set—
> Repeated, shift after shift—
> Day after day the same song—
> The same wearisome Song of the Drift.
>
> Run! Run! Run!
> Rush to the shaft the rich pay!
> Backward and forward in haste—

Watching the track by the way—
Run! Run! Run!
In a kind of nervous dread,
Fearing the "cap" that oft makes
A battering ram of your head;
This "curve"—that badly built "switch."
Look out! You know what they are.
Run! Run! thro' all the day long,
Sings this hasty Song of the Car.

Hoist! Hoist! Hoist!
No music there is in that sound!
Hoist! Hoist! Hoist!
Impatient voice underground!
You may wish your arm a crank
Attached to a water wheel!
With no aching bones at night,
Nor a weary frame to feel—
'Tis vain! Hoist away! Hoist!
The dirt comes heavy and moist,
And thirty buckets an hour
"Foot" to the tune of Hoist! Hoist!

Wash! Wash! Wash!
And rattle the rocks around,
Is the song the Dump-box sings,
So cheery the whole week round;
And on Sunday "clean me up"
And gather the precious "pay"
"Better the day—better the deed,"
Should read "Better the deed—the day!"
Now say, what have you "Wash'd up?"
Small wages—well never repine—
You know we'll do better next week!
And so ended the Song of the Mine.

One of the main problems in Barkerville, from the beginning, was that of communication and transport.

To meet it, Governor Douglas, at the very beginnings of the gold rush, began the construction of a road from the head of Harrison Lake, at Port Douglas, and thence to Lillooet. By this route the Fraser canyon was by-passed, but as it utilized a chain of lakes served by little steamboats, the handling costs—and delays—of consignments of goods sent to the interior grew out of all proportions.

It was decided, therefore, in 1862 to push a road through the canyon, and the first section out from Yale was built by members of the Royal

Engineers, a detachment of which had arrived late in 1858 to undertake public works projects and assist in maintaining law and order.

By 1864 the road extended right to Barkerville. Generally speaking, that section between Quesnel and Stanley is made up of the last link in the Cariboo Road. It branches off at Stanley, follows Lightning Creek, through Van Winkle, and comes into Barkerville from the south, ending close to St. Saviour's Church. Thus the main street of Barkerville is in reality the Cariboo Road. The road through the Devil's Canyon, and along Jack of Clubs Lake, and through the present town of Wells was not built until 1887.

With the completion of "the road", stage coaches and freight wagons replaced the packers, and the "cost of living" dropped considerably. The first man to start a restaurant at Richfield charged $2.50 per meal and in spite of a large patronage, soon went bankrupt. But with the completion of the road, prices tumbled, and the cost of a meal dropped to $1.00.

James Anderson, the poet, had this to say about it in one of his *Sawney's Letters,* written after the road was completed:

> You'd maybe like to ken what pay
> Miners get here for ilka day,
> Jist two pound sterling, sure as death—
> It should be four, atween us baith—
> For gin ye coont the cost o' livin'
> There's naething left to gang and come on;
> And should you bide the winter here,
> The shoppy-buddies 'll grab your gear,
> The little wark ane gets to do
> A' the lang dreary winter thro'.

Bill Phinney working rocker at Caledonian Claim

Barkerville, Richfield and Cameronton were not the only towns to spring up in the area. There was Marysville, on the Forest Rose claim, below Cameronton "near the meadows". This place was largely a "residential area". Cameronton was the location of the Royal Cariboo Hospital built in 1863 and later moved to Barkerville. On various other creeks and gulches in the vicinity were groups of stores and houses which became known as towns. On October 4, 1867, at a public meeting over 80 miners from Mosquito and Red Gulches were unanimous in the decision to call their new township on Mosquito "Centreville." By May, 1868, it was reported that 100 houses had been erected there. At the head of Conklin Gulch, south-east of Barkerville, a settlement sprang up known as Felixville, taking its name from the Felix Company which was well established there in mining.

When about 30 lots, with a frontage of 60 feet each had been sold at the mouth of Chisholm Creek (near Stanley) south-west of Barkerville, in 1870, the spot was called Gladstoneville, after the British statesman, and in 1877 at the time of the "quartz excitement" a small group of miners at Stouts Gulch called their place Carnarvontown.

As the roaring 60s faded into history, the more adventuresome prospectors turned away from Barkerville and headed towards the Omenica and the Cassiar districts to the north where new gold strikes were the lure. In the middle 1880s, it was to Granite Creek, near Princeton, and to the Kootenays and Rossland areas.

Barkerville, however, continued to hold its place as a gold camp; past old Cameronton, now covered with tailings, the firm of Kurtz & Lane, in the early 1870s, sank a shaft out on the "meadows" but all the effort put into it was fruitless, as water from Williams Creek and "slum"—a form of oozing mud—kept flowing into the hole to make work impossible.

An attempt was made at hard-rock mining above Richfield, and on the Bonanza Ledge at the head of Lowhee Creek. A stamp mill was erected at Richfield, but this development was overshadowed by the advent of the great hydraulic nozzles which blasted away the overburden to get at the gold lying at bedrock.

By this process the reason why Dutch Bill had proved so unsuccessful in his venture in the canyon was explained. Williams Creek had once flowed a few yards to the east of the present stream, and during the 1890s, the hydraulics blasted out a new canyon, removing millions of square yards of gravel to get down to the tertiary bed—the old course of Williams Creek. Conklins Gulch, Stouts Gulch, the Lowhee, and all the old workings were systematically cleaned out by the pressure of the hydraulic plants. The 1890s, indeed might be called "Cariboo's Hydraulic Era", for not only at Barkerville, but at Quesnelle Forks, Bullion, and other points in the gold region, vast networks of ditches were dug, and rivers diverted to bring water to the various mines.

Barnard's Cariboo Express rolls again

In 1888 a reduction works was established at Barkerville and one of the technicians associated with it was C. J. S. Baker, an Englishman better known as Seymour Baker.

Like Fred Wells, who was to enter the picture later, Baker had great faith in the Barkerville district as a quartz camp, but before anything could be done, several highly technical problems had to be solved. One of these was the dissolving of sulphates in solution, and in 1904 he solved this by developing a cyanide process. This, however, led to another problem, that of precipitating the gold from the cyanide solution. In the late 1920s this problem was solved elsewhere, and now, technically at least, it was possible to begin hard rock mining.

Seymour Baker's interests lay on Island Mountain, and he made many trips to England to try to raise capital to further the development work he had put into the property.

Now the picture switches back to 1862 and the discovery by Richard Willoughby of the Lowhee claim. Some of the nuggets he brought down to Barkerville had bits of quartz clinging to them and, although the presence of this foreign body was duly noted, none seemed to appreciate its significance.

Willoughby left the Cariboo to take up farming in the lower Fraser Valley at Chilliwack, and for nearly three-quarters of a century, nobody apparently followed up his clue. And then Al Sanders and Elmer Armstrong began poking little holes all over Cow Mountain, near the Lowhee claim, and uncovered a great vein of ore. A veteran prospector, Fred Wells, who had been in the Cariboo since 1922, convinced that a quartz property could be found, heard about the Sanders and Armstrong discovery and investigated the find. He was positive that the discovery was something important, and made a deal with the two partners, but he knew that finding a vein was one thing, and making a mine out of it was another.

Wells had been "in" on the development of several good properties in association with a surgeon-miner by the name of Dr. W. B. Burnett of Vancouver. Wells convinced the doctor that here was a mine and, with a few tools and a small crew, Wells started to drift a tunnel into the side of Cow Mountain to get under the surface showings of the Sanders vein.

When he had driven in 60 feet he cut a small vein which showed substantial values and several sizeable fragments of free gold. This "free gold" was the stimulus which raised several thousand hard-found dollars to keep the mine in operation.

Guided by what he found inside and outside, Wells recommended a new tunnel from the opposite side of Cow Mountain. A camp was set up and preparations were made to begin the work but, just at that moment, the Gold Commissioner from Barkerville arrived on the scene with instructions from the Minister of Mines, then the Hon. W. A. MacKenzie, ordering work to stop. At the same time, the minister telephoned Dr. Burnett stating the government could not permit the company to sell stock on the market for such a "wild venture" as this.

Peppery Fred Wells told the Gold Commissioner that unless he brought sufficient force to the mine to stop his eight men working, the order would not be obeyed, and he was backed up by Dr. Burnett who told him to keep working as long as there was money in the treasury.

The treasury was, in a few weeks, just like Mother Hubbard's cupboard —bare—and it couldn't be replenished because the government had forbidden the sale of shares. The situation became very desperate, but into the picture stepped O. H. Solibakke, of Seattle, who had worked in Alaska placer camps and was considered a "born salesman." After looking the property over, Solibakke went back to Seattle and raised the necessary capital.

Four years after beginning their work, the company, known as Cariboo Gold Quartz produced the first two gold bricks, and sent them down to Vancouver for display in a jewellery store window.

It was a magnificent accomplishment, and when Fred Wells died on September 1, 1956, at the age of 95 he was known throughout the province as "the Father of Lode Mining in the Cariboo."

Meanwhile, the success of the Cariboo Gold Quartz mine brought the district to the attention of the great Newmont Mining Corporation of New York who succeeded in making a deal with Seymour Baker for his Island Mountain property. The first payment was made, and Seymour Baker, his years of work now crowned with success, set sail for England. The second cheque for $33,000 arrived in Barkerville for him, but there was no one to pick it up. En route to England, Baker had died at sea.

In July, 1954, Cariboo Gold Quartz surprised everyone in the mining industry by buying out Island Mountain—indeed it had been supposed it would have been the other way around, with the great New York firm swallowing up the little B.C. company.

Island Mountain, which started operations in November, 1934, had produced up to the end of 1952 gold valued at $11,319,461 from 692,115 tons of ore. Cariboo Gold Quartz, which began a year earlier, had produced $18,224,801 from 1,348,292 tons. By the purchase of Island Mountain, Cariboo made their work much easier. Their claims surrounded the Island Mountain mine, and the deal meant that Cariboo, chronically short of money for development, acquired ready-made underground approaches to its own ore bodies. Island Mountain shafts went down 1,500 feet, compared with Cariboo's 500, and they went right up to the face of Cariboo's best ore at depth.

The mine is still in operation, and so for a hundred years now, the Barkerville area has been a producer of gold.

View of Wells

LIFE IN OLD BARKERVILLE

Almost without benefit of surveyor or town planner, Barkerville came into existence, and frankly, it looked as though it needed both. The nameless main street—which later served as the terminus of the Cariboo Wagon Road — was narrow and it was muddy. The buildings were jammed together as if every inch of land was worth a fortune, and no steps were taken to offset the ever-present danger of fire.

But for a town of its type, Barkerville possessed everything a man could ask for — except, possibly, some peace and quiet. There were laundries, bakers, barbers, churches, hotels, saloons, a theatre, breweries, restaurants, tinsmiths, a library, and a frontier newspaper.

The buildings were usually built on log posts, for you never knew when somebody's tailings would divert Williams Creek and send it flowing through town, or the seasonal flooding would make the stream a raging torrent. To get from one building to another each owner put a sidewalk in front of his business, but, unfortunately, they were set at different levels and so walking was unsafe. But, even at that, the sidewalks were infinitely better than the roadway below, which was always dirty, and none of the townspeople seemed to bother about repairing it, for, as they said, it was not up to them, it was a government problem.

The street was used for every conceivable purpose. Cattle were herded down it to the slaughter-house up by Richfield; there was horse racing down it, and, with the completion of the Cariboo Road, great freight wagons drawn by teams of oxen or mules, and F. J. Barnard's peerless six-horse stage coaches, added their contribution to keeping the road in a constant state of disrepair.

Busy street scene

In September, 1870, steps were taken to at least control the flooding from Williams Creek, when an abutment was run around the town. Parts of this wall can still be seen near the Diller claim at the south end of town. Another step taken was to build a series of three overpasses, similar to those now used in the cities by department stores to link parking facilities with the main store. One thing about these overpasses: they made wonderful observation points for the races!

The houses in the town were generally two storeys high, well lighted, and built of planed lumber and shake roofs. Some of them were painted, and a few papered within.

"Buildings in Barkerville," it has been noted," were the most elaborate and procured the highest rents of any in the Cariboo. When the government was opening an assay office in 1869 officials found that to rent a portion of a house in Barkerville would cost about $100 a month; to build one, $3,500. In Richfield, however, a suitable house would cost about $1500, or rented at rates from $20 to $50 a month."

Away from the "centre of town" the miners lived in cabins like the one James Anderson described in *Sawney's Letters*.

See yonder shanty on the hill?
'Tis but an humble biggin',
Some ten by six within the wa's—
Your head may touch the riggin',

The door stands open to the south,
The fire, outside the door;
The logs are chinket close wi' fog—
And nocht but mud the floor.

A knife an' fork, a pewter plate,
An' cup o' the same metal,
A teaspoon an' a sugar bowl,
A frying pan an' kettle;

The bakin' board hangs on the wa',
Its purposes are twa-fold—
For mixing bread wi' yeast or dough,
Or panning oot the braw gold!

A log or twa in place o' stools,
A ned withoot a hangin',
Are feckly a' the furnishing's
This little house belangin';

The laird and tenant o' this sty,
I canna name it finer,
Lives free an' easy as a lord,
Tho' but an "honest miner."

Miners' cabin, between Barkerville and Richfield

Business in the stores was done in a most informal manner, and any excuse to close down the shutters seems to have been a good one—just as any excuse for a party was.

> HALLO! OLD JACK'S ALIVE!
> JUST RETURNED FROM BEING ON A BENDER!
> Fully prepared to Repair all BOOTS and SHOES
> CHEAP FOR CASH. He kindly invites one and all,
> great and small, to give him a call.
> BARKERVILLE—next door to J. H. Todd's.
> (Advertisement in *Cariboo Sentinel*)

More sober in nature was Wellington Delaney Moses, the colored barber of Barkerville, whose place of business is now one of the most interesting exhibits in the Barkerville park. His advertisements in the *Sentinel* were always intriguing:

Moses boasted his "Hair Invigorator" guaranteed "the restoration of hair in one week." It must have had some degree of success, for a "to whom it may concern" card in the *Sentinel*, signed by three miners, states:

"This is to certify that from some cause or complaint of the head our hair commenced falling out so rapidly that we feared we should lose the whole. In this condition we went to W. D. MOSES and strange to relate in THREE applications of his wonderful Hair Restorative our hair became as strong as ever and is now soft and lively."

London-born Moses had been a prominent citizen of Victoria before joining the stampede to Williams Creek. In the Island city he had the first bath-tub the infant city had ever seen in his Pioneer Shaving Salon and Bathroom ("Private entrance for ladies.")

Moses' clients included the bearded miner, the hurdy gurdy girl, the dance hall girl, and the infamous James Barry, the murderer of Charles

Young and Old in Barkerville

Barkerville Library

Morgan Blessing.

W. D. Moses died in Barkerville on January 3, 1890, at the age of 74, and was probably buried in the old Cameronton cemetery, but no headstone marks his final resting place.

Quite often a merchant would have two occupations, besides doing a little bit of mining—or speculating—on the side. For instance: John Bowron, the librarian and postmaster, also cleaned pannings on commission; John Knott, the carpenter and head-board maker, who had a place next to the Barker claim, was also a stable-keeper. Perhaps the most intriguing "double business," though, was that advertised in the *Sentinel* on June 16, 1869, inserted by D. Lewis who

". . . begs leave to inform the ladies and gentlemen of Barkerville and vicinity that he has spared no pains in fitting up a Bathing Room for their accommodation, next door to Taylor's Drugstore, and hopes to merit a share of their patronage. He is also prepared to fill Teeth with Gold, Silver or Tin Foil, set in Teeth on pivots, repair Plates and extract Teeth. Having considerable experience in that line, Mr. Lewis feels assured of giving satisfaction."

Mr. Lewis was not the only one to go into the Bath House business. In June, 1865, Joseph Revis inserted this notice:

"THE ORIGINAL PIEMAN—Hot pies of the best description supplied to parties at their own residences at twenty-five cents each."

Unfortunately, the pie business was not as sugar-coated as he had hoped for, because on August 5 "the original pieman" had found a new outlet for his talents, which appeared under the title, "Original Notice."

"The undersigned begs leave to inform his friends and the public in general that he will open on Monday next a BATH HOUSE and will be prepared to give his patrons HOT and COLD BATHS in the best style. In consequence of the great influx of the Fair Sex he has determined to BRIGHTEN the UNDERSTANDING of Gentlemen who will favor him with a call; Blacking and Brushes, and an ample supply of Elbow Grease will always be found for that purpose. Charges to suit the depressed state of things. Gents who visit the Casinos will do well to give me a call; they will then be certain to make a SHINE.

Baths $1.00. Boots blacked 25 cents.
Joseph Revis
The Original Pieman."

Frank Laumeister, the man who had the unfortunate experience of introducing the use of camels on the Cariboo Road in 1860, only to have one shot by Grizzly Morris, and find himself in a lot of other difficulties because of the "ships of the desert," opened a store in Barkerville in June 1867. The firm of Oppenheimer Bros (one of the partners, David, became the second mayor of Vancouver) operated a large business establishment catering to the needs of the miner. Another was that of

J. H. Todd, a firm which is still in business today as one of the largest fisheries concerns on the coast. Roderick Finlayson, who with James Douglas, had founded Victoria, on behalf of the Hudson's Bay Company, opened a "Bay" store in Barkerville in June 1867.

By April 1867, the town was developing into quite a community, and on the 15th of that month, the *Sentinel* gave Barkerville a pat on the shoulders:

"The appearance of this town is improving steadily and there is not a building site left unoccupied. The town has extended right up to the China buildings at the upper end and cannot be extended down stream further unless by building on piles on account of the street being so high above the creek. The principal buildings of Cameronton have been moved to Barkerville . . ."

The story went on to list the types of business houses in town at that time: 12 saloons, 10 stores, 3 shoemakers, 3 restaurants, 3 lodging houses, 2 bank agencies, 1 printing office, 1 paint shop, 1 butcher's stall, 2 drug stores, 2 watchmakers, 2 breweries, 1 express office, 2 carpenters' shops, 1 post office, 1 public library, 1 clothing store and 1 public stable.

The many varied facets of business life in Barkerville are reflected in the town's newspaper, the *Cariboo Sentinel* which began publication on June 6, 1895. It was printed on the first press to reach this part of the country, one brought by Bishop Demers of the Roman Catholic Church to Victoria in 1843, and used to print the first book in what is now B.C., a work entitled *The Fraser River Mines Vindicated* by Alfred Waddington. It also printed the first newspaper in B.C., the French-language *Le Courier de la Nouvelle Caledonie*, and the first issues of the *Victoria Colonist*. This press is now one of the treasured possessions of the Sisters of St. Ann in Victoria. The price of the *Sentinel* was $1 a copy. At first it was a weekly, and thence became twice weekly, often closing up shop entirely for the winter.

Besides presenting the business cards of various enterprises up and down the Cariboo Road, as well as in Victoria, New Westminster, and even as far afield as San Francisco, it tells much about life in old Barkerville.

It carried the notices of the Library, funds for which were raised by public subscription, and was opened first in Cameronton by John Bowron in 1864. Three years later, when Cameronton had gone its course, it was moved to Barkerville where the reading room had "a well selected and diversified stock of books."

Bowron was one of the "cultural lions" of Barkerville, and with James Anderson, the poet, was one of the leaders of the Cariboo Amateur Dramatic Association who performed regularly in the Theatre Royal, which stood on the site of the present community hall and fire department buildings. To this theatre came groups of wandering minstrels and performers, but the most eagerly looked-forward-to performances were those written by Anderson.

Dentist Jones' "painless tooth extraction" parlor

There were other associations, too, like the Caledonian Benevolent Society, the Masonic Lodge, Cariboo Lodge No. 469, founded in 1868, and a Welsh organization. The Chinese Freemasons also functioned in Barkerville, just as they did at Quesnelle Forks.

Dentist Jones in action

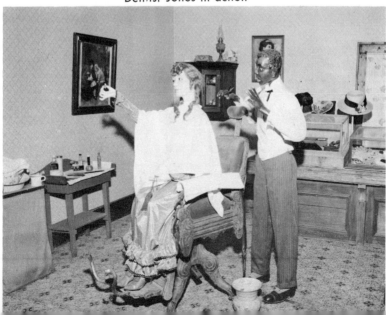

The Wake-Up Jake: Yesterday and Today

To take care of the "inner man" there were several restaurants both in Barkerville and Richfield, but the most famous was that started by Andrew Kelly with the intriguing name "Wake-Up Jake Restaurant and Bakery." The exact opening date of the Wake-Up Jake is not known, nor is any indication given as to whether there is a relationship between the Wake-Up Jake claim and the restaurant. The Wake-Up Jake advertised in the first issue of the Sentinel.

It was fairly large, having accommodation for private dining rooms, and although often called a "saloon" it was not the "drinking man's" idea of such a place. Today, it would be called a high-class restaurant where drinks can be obtained with meals.

The Wake-Up Jake has been rebuilt as a "coffee saloon" and one of its most prized possessions is a charcoal drawing of Barkerville before the fire, done by George Petherwick, which hung in the original Wake-Up Jake.

The drinking man was not without his saloons. These became the social centres of town; some of them were rough and ready, while others were eminently respectable. To these places, both good and bad, drifted the

Posed gambling picture taken about 1900

gamblers, of whom James Anderson says in his *Sawney Letters*:

There is a set o' men up here
Wha never work thro' a' the year,
A kind o' serpents, crawlin' snakes,
That fleece the miner o' his stakes;
They're Gamblers—honest men some say,
Tho' it's quite fair to cheat in play
IF IT'S NO KENT O'—I ne'er met
An honest man a Gambler yet!
O, were I judge in Cariboo
I'd see the laws were carried thro',
I'd hae the cairds o' every pack
Tied up into a gunny sack.
Wi' a' the gamblers chained tegither
And banish'd frae the creek forever.
But, Sawney, there's anither clan,
There's name o' them I'd ca' a man,
They ca' them "jumpers"—its my belief
That jumper is Chinook for thief:—
They jump folk's claims and jump their lots,
They jump the very pans and pots;
But wait a wee—for a' this evil—
Their friend 'll jump them.
He's the devil.

There were several attempts to chase them out of town, the first being instigated by the Rev. R. C. Lundin Brown who lived under great hardship in Cameronton in 1862-63. As Bancroft said, "he attacked the gamblers in their den, but was ultimately obliged to withdraw from the field unsuccessfully."

Another attempt, with at least temporary or partial success, was noted in the *Sentinel* for November 28, 1868:

"There has been a great deal of argument as to whether public gambling in Cariboo ought to be prohibited or not, and up to last week no attempt has been made to stop it, so long as the tables were not set in the public bar rooms, and no disturbance ensued; in fact it always seemed to be understood that the authorities would not interfere unless on the complaint of private individuals. This week, however, things are changed, the district magistrate having instructed the constables to see that no gambling is carried on in any room attached to a public saloon. And everything is now silent and dark where formerly, night after night, the tables were surrounded by anxious groups in pursuit of fortune. In connection with this subject, many parties are of the opinion that gambling ought to be licensed. If it is not carried on in public, they say, it will be in private; consequently the government would be perfectly justified in exacting a tax which would largely assist the revenue, both directly and indirectly."

Following this blow to their profession, many gamblers packed their bags and left town, some for White Pine, a new silver field in California. James Anderson "mourned" their departure in this song, entitled *Come Back Faro* set to the air *Peter Gray*.

I'll sing you now a mournful song,
All of a fine old man,
Who liv'd some years in Cariboo,
All by his sleight of han'.
(*Chorus*)
Come back, Faro, come back, Faro, pray,
Or I'll sing toorah la de O!
Sing toorah la de A!
Altho' he lay in his bed all day,
He was wide awake at night;
And when the luck was on his side,
His face beam'd with delight.
I've often watched his little game,
And even been case-keeper;
And tho' his eyes were pretty sharp,
I've sometimes nailed a sleeper.
At times he'd grumble of hard luck
And say he'd ne'er a dollar—
Yet he lived jolly as a lord,
And wore a paper collar.
Ah, many a time he found me grub,
When I had ne'er a red—
Now I must work ten hours a day
Since good old Faro's dead.
But what is worse, I dare not dance,
Nor squeeze a little paw—
I'll tell the reason, but don't "ment'ch"
I cannot "shoot my jaw."
Some say old Faro was a rogue,
Tho' tis not my belief;
But if he were—then I am sure
Young Lansquenet's a thief.
Whate'er you were, old Faro dear,
I'll not defame the dead—
Your ghost might haunt me some cold night,
And "freeze me out" in bed.
(*Chorus*)
Goodbye, Faro goodbye, old Faro, dear.
And may you strike it in White Pine
And may we strike it here.

33

Barnard's Express (the B.X.) office

34

For those who were not gambling or dancing, there were quiet card games in the bar-rooms, often to see who would pay for the drinks. There was euchre, and, as James Anderson notes, a game called *Sinch*.

Now kind friends, attention, and list to my song,
'Tis neither too short, nor yet very long—
It's all of a little game play'd on this creek,
Ev'ry hour of the day, and ev'ry day in the week—
Some play for pastime, and some play for beer,
Some play because a dear barmaid is near;
But only the Scotchmen can play the game right,
For Sawney hates "sinching" but loves to get tight!
(*Chorus*)
Sinch, sinch, who'll take a hand,
Sinch, sinch, sinch, who will play;
Drink brandy, or rum or lager who may
Sinch for hot whiskey, hot whiskey I'll play.

Now give us two beans and throw round for the deal,
This game's on the square, boys, so no one may steal;
Ah, 'tis my sell, now who will buy me—
Stow Sawney says "one" while Paddy says "three".
I can make three, myself, I don't know what to do,
But I'll take the beans, Pat, seeing it's you;
So Paddy gets "sinched"—he has only Jack High—
While Sawney says "barkeep, hot whiskey I'll tak'!"
(*Chorus*: Sinch, sinch, etc.)
Then we play'd to sinch Sawney, but the rogue he was shy,
And long ere each game closed, auld Sawney was dry;
But after ten rounds his eyelids were clinched
And Sawney, unconscious, was thoroughly "sinch'd."
We play'd all that night, and next morning was found
On a bench by the stove Sawney, sleeping quite sound—
Till a fall on the floor half awakened the Scot—
And he hicupp'd out "barkeep, gie more whiskey hot."
(*Chorus*: Sinch, sinch, etc.)
There's something I see, I can't well explain
How some men can drink, who ne'er treat again—
And breakfast at home on a chip of dry toast
To dine at a restaurant on pudding and roast;
While others play billiards, and sport
Without visible means of support—
And often play sinch without even a red
And sometimes, like Sawney, go drunk to their bed.
Sinch, sinch, who hasn't been sinched,
Sinch'd, sinch'd in a dollar or two—
The barkeep, the baker, the miner, the Jew,
Have each one been sinched by rough Cariboo.

The saloons were the headquarters for nearly all activities in town. All conceivable anniversaries were celebrated and sometimes an exhibition of magic or boxing was staged. By the middle of 1869 there were as many as 18 saloons in Barkerville and Richfield. They had wonderful names, too, such as Go-at Them; the Gazelle, Parlor, El Dorado, Billiard, the Fashion, to name a few. Again, James Anderson, and *Sawney*:

> I kent a body make a strike—
> He looked a little lord!
> An' had a clan o' followers
> Amang a needy horde.
>
> Whane'er he'd enter a saloon
> You'd see the barkeep smile—
> His Lordship's humble servant he
> Without a thocht a' guile!
>
> A twal' months past an' a' is gane
> Baith freends an' brandy—bottle;

Street scene, note raised sidewalks

An' noo the puir soul's left alane
Wi' nocht to weet his throttle!

The "largest and most complete Saloon in British Columbia" was Barry & Adler's Fashion Saloon "consisting of three large separate apartments, viz., Card Room, Bar Room and Billiard Saloon, containing three superb billiard tables." The Snug invited friends to "drop in and sample their ales, wines and liquors, the quality of which they flatter themselves will suit the taste of the most fastidious." The Crystal Palace Saloon, run by Mundorf & Co., invited the public to "come and enjoy the light fantastic." For special events, seats in the saloons sold for as much as $2 each, but on ordinary evenings there was no "cover charge." There was very little trouble in the saloons, and when a fight did break out, it was usually a fist fight. The gunslinger of the TV western was not to be found.

Prize fights were popular and bouts were well attended, with the betting usually pretty brisk. Another favourite sport was horse-racing, but races were infrequent. For universal popularity, though, you couldn't beat stone-throwing, which seems to have been indulged in by all, and the rivalry between friends as to who could throw a stone the furthest was high.

BAR ROOM SONG

Air: *For A' that an' a' that.*)
Hurrah for rum and whiskey hot
That fires the brain, an' a' that!
The sober man, we pass him by,
We dare be drunk, for a' that!
For a' that, an' a' that!
The mind is but the weak man's plea;
The muscle's man for a' that!
See ye, that miner—in his cups—
Wi' sou'thers broad an' a' that!
Wha calls himsel' a man o' micht,
O' principle, an' a' that!
The man that's on the shoulder, he
Keeps his ain side for a' that.
Tho' gold may buy a man good claes,
May steal his sense, an' a' that!
It's only Muscle wha can win
His battles ain, an' a' that!
For a' that, an' a' that!
Their billiard balls, an' a' that!
When Muscle takes the cue he breaks
Baith heads an' balls, an' a' that!
Then let us pray that come it may,
"As soon it will" for a' that!

37

Micht shall be richt the warld o'er
In dance, saloon, an' a' that
For a' that, an' a' that!
Hurrah for hell, an' a' that!
Let's drink and fight and gouge and bite,
We're gentlemen for a' that!
Rejoice, young man, when in your prime,
Live fast, get drunk, an' a' that!
Auld age, should you e'er live to see't
Will put an end to a' that!
For a' that, an' a' that!
Ye'll pay the debt for a' that!
When nature's sel' demands o' you
A true account o' a' that!

And then, there were the dance hall girls.

THE DANCING GIRLS OF CARIBOO

(Air: *Young man from the countree.*)
We are dancing girls in Cariboo,
And we're liked by all the men,
In gum boots and a blanket coat—
And e'en the upper ten!
We all of us have swee-eet hearts,
But the dearest of all to me,
Is that young man who wistfully
Casts those sheep's eyes at me!
(*Chorus*: Is that young man, etc.)
O ev'ry night at eight o'clock,
We enter the saloon—
Altho' it may be vacant then
'Tis crowded very soon.
Then all the boys they stare at us,
But we do not mind that so,
Like those four and twenty Welshmen,
All sitting in a row.
(*Chorus*: Like those four, etc.)
O what a charming thing it is,
To have a pretty face—
To know that one can kill as well
In calico as lace;
We steal the hearts of everyone,
But the dearest of all to me,
Is that dear boy with the curly head
Who loves me faithfully!
(*Chorus*: Is that dear boy, etc.)

To all the boys of Cariboo
This moral—which is right—
From the dancing gals of Cariboo
You may see on any night—
"Before we either give our hearts,
Or yet our sympath-ee,
You must be like this dear young man
Who spends his all on me!"
(*Chorus*: You must be, etc.)

A new and far different type of dance hall girl appeared on the scene in 1866, when Madame Fannie Bendixen brought in the first of the

Madame Bendixon standing on balcony of Hotel de France

hurdy-gurdy girls from San Francisco for her Bella Union Saloon. The *Sentinel* has left us this description of the "hurdy."

HURDY GURDY DAMSELS

"There are three descriptions of the above-named "ladies" here; they are unsophisticated maidens of Dutch [*sic*] extraction, from 'poor but honest parents' and morally speaking, they really are not what they are generally put down for. They are generally brought to America by some speculating, conscienceless scoundrel of a being commonly called a 'Boss Hurdy.' This man binds them in his service until he has received about a thousand percent for his outlay. The girls receive a few lessons in the terpsichorean art, are put into a kind of uniform, generally consisting of a red waist, cotton print skirts and a half-mourning headdress resembling in shape the top-knot of a male turkey; this uniform gives them quite a gortesque [*sic*] appearance. Few of them speak English but they soon pick up some popular vulgarisms, and like so many parrots they use them indiscriminately on all occasions; if you bid one of them good morning your answer will likely be 'itsh sphlaid out' or 'you bet your life.'

"The Hurdy style of dancing differs from all other schools. If you ever saw a ring of bells in motion, you have the exact position these young ladies are put through during the dance; the more muscular the partner, the nearer the approximation of the ladies pedal extremities to the ceiling, and the gent who can hoist his 'gal' the highest is considered the best dancer; the poor girls as a general thing earn their money very hardly.

HURDY FIDDLERS

"This class of musicians (pardon the misnomer) have also a school of their own, in which melody and euphony have no part. Noise is the grand object. The one who can make the most noise is (amongst the hurdy artists) considered the most talented. Sometimes to increase the power of an orchestra (which seldom consists of more than two violins— more properly 'fiddlers' in this case) they sing and play, and in passing on Broadway, Barkerville, in the evening you may hear them letting off steam as if their lungs were made of cast iron and the notes forged with a sledge hammer."

Anderson, of course, could not let such a notable event as the hurdies go unnoticed, and in fact wrote two ditties about them. This one is from *Sawney's Letters* and the air is *Green Grow the Rushes*.

> Last simmer we had lassies here
> Frae Germany—the hurdies, O!
> And troth I wot, as I'm a Scot,
> They were the bonnie hurdies, O!
> There was Kate and Mary, blithe and airy,
> And dumpy little Lizzy, O!
> An' ane they ca'd the Kangaroo,
> A strappin', rattlin' hizzy, O!
> They danced at nicht in dresses light,
> Frae late until the early, O!
> But oh! their hearts were hard as flint,
> Which vexed the laddies sairly, O!
> The Dollar was their only love,
> And that they lo'ed fu' dearly, O!
> They didna care a flea for men,
> Let them coort hooe'er sincerely, O!
> They left the creek wi' lots o' gold,

Danced frae oor lads sae clever, O!
My blessing's on their "sour kraut" heads,
Gif they stay awa for ever, O!
                    (Chorus)
Bonnie are the hurdles, O!
The German hurdy-gurdies, O!
The daftest hour that e'er I spent
Was dancin' wi' the hurdies, O!

And here is an excerpt from his second song, entitled *The Flower of Germany*, set to the air *Captain With His Whiskers*.

You may fancy ballet dancers,
In their snowy clouds of lace,
My Katie in her calico,
For me has ev'ry grace;
Her step is lighter than the deer
Upon the heather bell,
And sweeter is her breath than those
Sweet violets in the dell,
And she trips it light and gay,
Like a fairy in the ring,
And her waltzing smoothly glides
Like a bird upon the wing;
So sing of "Annie Laurie"
She is rather Scotch for me—
I sing "saur kraut and lager beer"
And "Ye Flow'r of Germanie."

Mrs. Bendixon's enterprise proved so successful that on March 16, 1867, competition arrived on the scene, as reported in the *Sentinel*.

"Last Monday an addition was made to the number of our professors of the "light fantastic" by the arrival of eight German damsels, direct from the Bay City, who are under an engagement with Messrs. Barry & Adler of the Fashion Saloon of this place. We believe they will be introduced to the 'boys' next Saturday night when the ball will open for the season."

The next issue of the *Sentinel* described the ball:

"Messrs. Adler & Barry's large saloon was crowded on Saturday night with the 'boys' who had collected from every corner of the creek, to have a peep at the 'hurdies' who made their debut on that occasion. As a matter of course, many of the 'boys' were unable to resist the temptation of indulging in the 'mazy dance' while their 'chums' crowded around them in a circle and applauded their efforts in a most demonstrative manner. So great was the noise at times that it was next to impossible for the leader of the orchestra to keep anything like regularity in the management of the dance and the consequence was an occasional 'break down' in the figure which was always hailed with an uproarious burst of appro-

Barkerville, before the fire

bation on the part of the spectators, much to the evident discomfiture of
the ladies, who were doubtless unaccustomed to such noisy scenes, or still
more to the peculiar fashion adopted by the 'boys' of throwing them up
a foot or two from the floor at the end of every figure."

Unknown to the management at this time, or to the miners who tossed
them about, one of these eight hurdies was to spell the doom of Barkerville.
It came at 2.30 p.m. on September 16, 1868. Legend has it that a miner,
bent on stealing a kiss from a hurdy as she was pressing her dress at the
back of the saloon, knocked over a stove pipe. And Barkerville burned.
In an hour and 20 minutes only one building remained.

Frederick Dally, Barkerville's photographer, has left us a graphic account
of the fire and its aftermath. He later wrote this account, edited by Gordon
R. Elliott:

"By the number of stove-pipes very close together coming through the
wooden roofs of the buildings at every height and in every direction, that
were sending forth myriads of sparks numbers of which were constantly
alighting on the roofs where they would remain many seconds before going
out, and from the dryness of the season, I came to the conclusion that
unless we shortly had rain or snow to cover the roofs, for they remain
covered with snow all winter, that the town was doomed . . .

"The morning of the fire was bright and clear and the sluice boxes . . .
bore traces of a hard frost as the icicles that were depending on the flumes

were two or three yards in length . . . Although trade was somewhat dull, still it was ready and profitable. . . . Little did I think that in less than two hours, not a vestige of the town would remain but a burning mass of ruins. . . .

"I seated myself in a chair and again meditated on the probability of a fire when I heard several running on the plank sidewalk and heard one exclaim, 'Good God! What is up?' I ran instantly to see the cause of the alarm and to my astonishment beheld a column of smoke rising from the roof of the saloon adjoining the steward's house. I saw the fire had a firm hold of the building and, as there was not water to be had, I felt certain that the town would be destroyed. So I collected as much of my . . . goods as possible together, and hastened with them to the middle of the creek, and left them there whilst I made several journeys after other goods. . . . Flames quickly set the opposite building, the Bank of British Columbia, in flames.

"So the fire travelled at the same time up and down both sides of the street . . . and although my building was nearly fifty yards away from where the fire originated, in less than 20 minutes it, together with the whole lower part of town, was a sheet of fire, hissing and crackling and roaring furiously. There were, in a store not far from my place, fifty kegs of blasting powder and had that not been removed at the commencement of the fire and put down a dry shaft, most likely not a soul would have been left alive of the number that was present. Blankets and bedding were

After the fire

seen to be sent at least 200 feet high when a number of coal oil tins, 5 gallons, exploded and the top of one of the tins was sent five miles and dropped at the sawmill on Grouse Creek.

"Every person was thinking of his own property and using desperate efforts to save it, and some not placing it sufficiently far out of reach of the element had all consumed, and others again had taken it so far that during the time they were away trying to save more property, Chinamen and others were stealing from them as fast as they could carry it away. One stout Chinaman showing too many creases about him that did not look quite natural, the police made him strip, and off came six shirts, two pairs of drawers, three pairs of trousers, etc. Another, two coats, three shirts, and two pairs of trousers. Another had hidden away behind the false canvas wall of his house, over one thousand dollars' worth of flour, rice, boots, etc., and every useful article usually sold by storekeepers in the mines.

"The town was divided by the 'Barker' flume, crossing it at a height of about fifty feet, and as it was carrying all the water that was near, it kept the fire at bay for a short time from the upper part of the town. But the hot wind soon drove those that were standing on it away. The fire then quickly caught the other half of the buildings, also the forest on the mountain ridge at the back. And as the sun set behind the mountain, the grandeur of the scene will not be quickly forgotten by those who noticed it.

"And then the cold frosty wind came sweeping down the canyon,

The smouldering embers of Barkerville

blowing without sympathy on the houseless and distressed sufferers, causing the iron-hearted men to mechanically raise the small collars on their coats (if they had been so fortunate as to save one) as protection against it. Household furniture of every description was piled up alongside the creek, and the people were preparing to make themselves as comfortable for the night, under the canopy of heaven, as circumstances would allow. And in the early morning, as I passed down the creek, I saw strong men rise from their hard cold stones, having wrapped up in a pair of blankets, cramped with cold and in great pain, until a little exercise renewed life into their systems."

The sole building to survive the holocaust was Scott's Saloon, and it remained until the middle 1930s when it was torn down.

The day following the fire the town began to rise from its ashes, and the *Sentinel*, on the 22nd reported:

"Already there are over thirty houses standing in symmetrical order on the old site, and the foundation of several others laid, and many more would yet have been in the course of erection were it possible to obtain carpenters and tools. . . . The town when rebuilt will present a much more uniform and pleasant appearance. By the regulations of the local authorities, in concurrence with the people, the mainstreet has been increased in width fifteen feet and the sidewalks fixed at regular and uniform grade. Vacancies which were originally intended for cross streets, but occupied by sufferance, are now to be left open, and altogether the new town will be much more convenient for business, and will be a decided improvement over the old; and we would not much wonder if in the course of a few years time many who are now heavy losers will cease to regret the conflagration of 1868."

But Barkerville's glory had passed. One of the signs of the times appeared in the *Sentinel* for July 14, 1869:

"TERPSICHOREAN DECADENCE—One of the popular institutions of Barkerville is about to disappear. Sterling's Terpsichorean academy [the El Dorado Saloon] will shortly lose its principal attraction by the departure of its lady professors, who contemplate returning to their wonted homes and these are not in British Columbia. Cariboo toes are not so light and fantastic as they used to be, neither are there quite so many of them. The filthy lucre becomes more precious with its scarcity, and the dance now most appreciated is that which is induced by the monotonous music of the water as it runs over a glittering dump-box. The temples of Apollo and Terpsichore are losing their devotees, who now evince an increasing disposition to frequent those of Mammon. In the meantime, subscriptions for the proposed building of a church are small and few. 'Whither are we drifting?' ".

Stirling's El Dorado Saloon held out until September 1, 1873, when it was sold at auction, and the Wake-Up Jake Restaurant and Bakery closed its doors on June 30, 1873.

45

Davis, or Cornish water wheel and flume (above) hydraulic operation at Morning Star Claim

But during the period of reconstruction following the fire one of the busiest men in town was Johnnie Knott, sometimes spelled Nott.

Knott was one of the town's carpenters, and although much of his handiwork stands today, fate played a dirty trick on him.

Several of the headboards in the old Cameronton cemetery are his work (they can be identified by the initials JK at the base) and usually he wasn't paid for them, but sent the markers along in lieu of flowers. But Johnnie took particular pains with one of them, designed for himself. He also made his own coffin, and in this he was buried. But before friends got around to erecting his headboard, a nephew arrived in town, perhaps with the hope that the old carpenter had amassed a fortune, but, alas, there was none. Disappointed, and bitter, the nephew sold the tombstone to the relatives of Samuel Shoemaker, who died at Willow River on October 1, 1895. It is said the nephew got a fancy price for it, but Johnnie's grave is unmarked. The Knott *cum* Shoemaker headboard has been removed from the cemetery due to old age and decay, but can still be seen in a more permanent setting.

One of Johnnie's jobs was the building of the Barkerville Hotel, and he appears to have operated it in 1869. Later it passed into the hands of the Kelly family, and in the popular mind became known as the Kelly Hotel.

Andrew Kelly had operated a lodging house at the "the lower end of

Johnnie Butt's carpenter shop

The Kelly Hotel

Barkerville" in which he was succeeded by Mrs. W. Michael in 1871.
Kelly thereupon purchased the Hotel de France from Julia Picot, who had
taken over the establishment in 1869 from Lecuyer & Brun. Kelly
announced the re-opening of the hotel on June 26, 1871. The adjoining
Hotel de France burned in 1948, and all that remains is the dining room,
now known as Kelly's Saloon.

The paintings on the wall, the gas lamp, and the glass mirrors over the

Kelly Saloon

bar, in this "reconstructed saloon" are "original Barkerville pieces". The old nickelodeon against the wall still works, but unfortunately a wheel has slipped somewhere along the line and nobody knows what it used to play. Now when the crank is turned, it gives out one of the loudest noises in the Cariboo.

Today the blacksmith has practically vanished, his place taken by the

Sandy McArthur's blacksmith shop

motor mechanic and the welder, but here in Barkerville Alex "Sandy" McArthur's smith shop has been preserved. It originally stood on a back street near the stables and warehouses. Note the axle-grease box amid the pile of horseshoes and other bits of paraphernalia "in studied disorder." Like the smithy, axle-grease has gone by the boards, and this box, with its fresh-appearing labels, is one of the most prized possessions of those reconstructing Barkerville to what it looked like during its golden era. The old buildings were there, but the little things, like axle-grease boxes, common enough in their time, had vanished. As one of those in charge of the reconstruction once said, "garbage is our greatest problem." So note the little things in Barkerville as well as the big, for like the axle-grease box they are the result of painstaking searches, and a good deal of luck.

The Nicol Hotel came into being when three buildings were joined

The Nicol Hotel

together in 1898 by Tom Nicol, and this was the "last saloon" in Barker-ville. The beer parlour, as saloons later came to be called, closed in the middle 1940s, and Barkerville went dry for the first time in its long history.

The Masonic Hall, Cariboo Lodge No. 469, dates back only to 1936, but its traditions go back much further. The first hall was opened on June 24, 1868, and that night the lodge brothers held a St. John's Day dinner in the Wake-Up Jake, but a few months later, it was destroyed in the great fire which swept through town. By February 1869 a new hall, larger than the original one, was being built, but it was doomed to die a fiery death in 1936.

With the opening up of the Cariboo Gold Quartz Mine in 1933, Barkerville became the scene of feverish activity. While the new townsite of Wells was being developed, Barkerville became "home" to hundreds of miners.

Barkerville general store

THE LAW

IN COMPARISON WITH other rip-roaring gold camps of the period, Barkerville was remarkably peaceful as far as crime was concerned. There is a story about Matthew Baillie Begbie, the first judge in British Columbia, which might point out one of the reasons why it was unnecessary to go about armed, even in the early days.

On his first visit to Barkerville he took a walk out to the meadows, and as he was always interested in natural history, he picked up a bunch of wild oats and brought them back into town as evidence of the fertility of the soil.

"What's that you have, judge?" asked a rough and ready miner.

"Wild oats," replied Begbie.

"Sowing or reaping them, judge?" he was asked.

"Neither, my friend. The man who comes to this country to sow his wild oats will find so many difficulties besetting him that he will quickly abandon the project; you understand!"

Despite the great influx of miners into Cariboo, including many who had been "invited" to leave San Francisco by the vigilantes under the shadow of a few yards of hemp, there was very little crime in Barkerville.

Begbie's justice was stern, but perhaps another reason was the remoteness of the country and the utter dependency upon the one north-and-south road for access to and from the coast.

Another reason was the incorruptible police force of Chartres Brew. (See Cameronton cemetery chapter.)

Begbie had been a lawyer in London, and was chosen by the Colonial Secretary, Sir Edward Bulwer Lytton, possibly better known as the novelist and author of *Last Days of Pompeii*, for the position. By his choice, Lytton certainly selected the right man at the right time. He was unorthodox and he was tough.

"If a man insists on behaving like a brute, after a fair warning, and won't quit the Colony, treat him like a brute and flog him."

He was often in "hot water" with public opinion, but it cannot be denied that "Begbie justice" kept law and order on the creeks. He was

Judge Begbie

51

given the epithet "hanging judge" but as Gordon Elliott pointed out in his history of Quesnel it "came not from the fact that he condemned many to death, for he did not, but rather from the way he might speak to criminals or the way he might admonish a jury. At one time when the jury brought in a verdict of manslaughter at a trial where a gunman had been proved guilty of deliberate murder, the Judge is reputed to have turned his wrath on the group and said:

"Had the jury performed their duty I might now have the painful satisfaction of condemning you to death, and you, gentlemen of the jury, you are a pack of Dalles horse thieves, and permit me to say, it would give me great pleasure to see you hanged, each and every one of you, for declaring a murderer guilty of only manslaughter."

At one of his "circuit court" sessions in 1865 there was only one criminal case brought before him and the culprit pleaded guilty. Judge Begbie looked at the prisoner and said, "Go, and sin no more."

Most of the cases brought to court were purely civil actions—disputes over claims, etc., or, as the *Sentinel* put it, those who had "worshipped too long at the shrine of Bacchus." Chinese would often go at each other with knives, shovels and anything that happened to be handy, but strangely, no one seemed to hurt the other very seriously. A few days in jail seemed to calm them down for a while, and then they would be at it again.

There were two jails in the area, one at Richfield and the other at Barkerville. Nobody knows today exactly where the Barkerville jail was located but it probably was at the north end of town, and not necessarily on the main street. The Richfield jail was close to the courthouse. The Barkerville "hoosegow" has been described as "a small but comfortable log building" and contained two cells. By 1870 it had fallen into disuse and Chartres Brew bought it for $186.50.

While there were no murders in Barkerville itself, there were a couple in the area, and the first of these occurred at Richfield in 1863. The story was told by J. B. Leighton, one of the last of the 1860'ers, and concerns a Mrs. Hetherington, better known as the "Scotch lassie" because of the strong Gaelic flavour to her speech. She came to B.C. in 1859 and after a year or two in Yale on the lower Fraser went to Cariboo.

"It appeared from what she told about herself," wrote Leighton in 1935, "that she had married a drunkard. He had insisted on her drinking, and had gone from bad to worse. Eventually she left him and was now on her own.

"One day during the season of 1863 the town of Richfield was startled by the report that the Scotch Lassie had been murdered in her cabin. The little village was thrown into an uproar of excitement. The coroner, Dr. Thomas Bell, a Fellow of the Royal College of Surgeons, took charge. He selected a jury of six men from among the crowd present. After looking the body over he reported that the woman had been smothered while in a high state of intoxication. No bruises or marks of any kind were found on the body.

"Mr. Angus Johnson was chosen as foreman of the jury. He led them into the cabin where the body lay with a towel over its face. Johnson lifted the towel, and there lay Jessie Hamilton, his mother's housemaid, still retaining some of her good looks.

"The coincidence of this sudden discovery was a decided shock to young Johnson. Although he was able to give witness of much of the past life of the unhappy girl, nothing was found to warrant the arrest and trial of any particular malefactor.

"The girl was buried near the cabin on the hillside, and the incident was quickly forgotten in the prevailing lust for sudden wealth. Only young Johnson never forgot the shock he received when he saw the girl's face for the last time."

The most famous case in the Williams Creek area was that of James Barry, charged with the murder of Charles Morgan Blessing. Around his case has grown this legend.

Blessing, 33, was the son of a wealthy Boston family who had followed the will-o-the-wisp of gold through the California rush, and then up into British Columbia. On a stick-pin he carried a unique nugget, one in the shape of a human head, but unfortunately the jeweller who mounted it had put it in upside down.

Grave of Chartres Brew

53

Enroute to the Cariboo he fell in with Wellington Delaney Moses, the Negro barber, and the pair became good friends. At Quesnel, where they arrived on May 28, 1866, they met a gambler by the name of James Barry, who was intrigued not only with Blessing's stick pin, but with his roll of $20 Bank of British Columbia notes.

Blessing, it seems, was in no hurry to get to Barkerville, but Moses was, and the pair parted company with the barber going on alone. A few days later, Blessing and Barry took to the dusty road—and for Blessing it was the road to doom. Near Pinegrove—a couple of miles east of present-day Wingdam—Blessing was shot in the back of the head. The crime went unnoticed for several weeks, although Moses was, for some strange reason, suspicious that something was wrong, especially when he saw Barry wearing Blessing's stickpin.

As soon as the body was discovered, Barry skipped town and nearly got away with it, but was captured at Yale, and on the evidence of Moses and the little golden stick-pin, was sent to the gallows.

In front of the courthouse a scaffold was erected for a double hanging, the platform being shared by an Indian who had been convicted of murdering a white man down at Soda Creek.

Most of the cases brought to court were tried before the gold commissioner, and these were mining disputes. The first of these to serve on Williams Creek was Thomas Elwyn, a popular man, but whose income from the government was scarcely enough to keep body and soul together. Elwyn did a little mining, and struck it lucky, and reported to the government: "The claim has of late become so valuable that I cannot in justice to myself abandon it." The next year, however, Elwyn was back in government service.

Others who succeeded Elwyn included Peter O'Reilly, H. M. Ball, Chartres Brew and John Bowron.

Gold Commissioner's office

THE FIRE DEPARTMENT

THE FIRE WHICH SWEPT through Barkerville on that fateful September afternoon of 1868, taught the townsfolk a lesson; they had to give more serious attention to the Williams Creek Fire Brigade.

The Brigade had been formed under a Mr. McNehanie in April 1867, but it had no equipment other than buckets, and so after the embers had died out, Isaac Oppenheimer set to work to re-organize the company. Through the offices of his brother, David, a piece of equipment was obtained in San Francisco, but it was a long time in coming.

However, using what equipment he could get together, Oppenheimer whipped his men into shape and on May 24th, 1869, "about seven o'clock, the W.C.F.B. turned out to drill. This was the first drill and," said the *Sentinel*, "like all first attempts, was a little imperfect, but quite perfect enough to give assurance that with a little practice we shall soon have a most efficient body of firemen. Captain Oppenheimer evidently understands the duties of his position thoroughly."

One of its members was James Anderson, the "bard of Barkerville," who wrote this song which was sung in the old Theatre Royal where it

Williams Creek Fire Brigade on parade

proved quite a hit. It was written to the air *Riding on a Railroad Car.*

> Oh! I belong to the Fire Brigade
> "And don't you think I ought to!"
> A prettier boy was never made,
> My uniform I bought too!
> My shirt of wool, an' scarlet dye,
> And pants and belt agree—
> With helmet and badge on that.
> Of the W.C.F.B.
>   (*Chorus*: With helmet and badge, etc.)
> We have an engine house for show
> A stable—but no 'oss
> Which grieves me very much indeed,
> And makes me rather cross.
> We are to have tanks on the hill
> And trust our luck for warter—
> Were the choice mine, I'd have engine
> And hook to Heave n' 'arter.
>   (*Chorus*: Were the choice mine, etc.)
> I know hydraulic is the thing,
> To break a gravel bank—
> And very soon would drown a fire—
> Tho' I don't like the "tank"
> But I'll still muster with the boys,
> For we should pull together
> "No frog or mouse" shall burn a house
> Our Fire Brigade forever.
>   (*Chorus*: No frog or mouse, etc.)

Scarcely had ten days gone by before the W.C.F.B. was called into action to fight a bush fire near Von Volkenburgh's slaughter house up near Richfield. The fire broke out on June 4 and the owners of the threatened establishment inserted a card next day in the *Sentinel* as a "tribute of our gratitude and sincere thanks for their heroic and persistent efforts in subduing the fire in the forest immediately adjacent to our Slaughter house and corrals, thereby saving our property, valued at $5,000 from imminent destruction."

The following week, a reader in Richfield poo-pooed the thought that the Williams Creek Fire Brigade was "heroic and persistent, and said "the hand of Providence was with us, not the Barkerville Fire Brigade."

A reader who signed himself Dominie Sampson of Slum Gulch, took pen in hand to write a letter to the editor about this:

"Sir," he wrote, "my leisure hours are devoted principally to the study of matters theological, and I should like to be made acquainted with your correspondent, as I believe I can convince him that since the time when our Saviour was on earth, Providence has not vouchsafed to work any miracles at all—not even for endangered cities of far more importance than Richfield."

And that was that.

The leather hose arrived in July 1869, but the carriage for the hose did not arrive until October 1871. From time to time fires would break out, and the church bell and the fire bell would sound the warning and the volunteer fireman would race for the reels.

This equipment, with the locally made hooks and ladders, is still in use today. The original leather hoses, of course, have gone, and a modern siren sounds the alarm.

The Chinese community had their own fire fighting equipment, which for ingenuity couldn't be beaten. It consisted of a fire pump constructed of hollow bamboo and was operated by hand. It was designed to hurl streams of water from buckets on the ground onto the flames on the roof-tops.

Theatre Royal

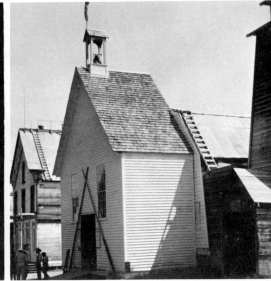

Trapper Dan's Cabin

CHINATOWN

To the white miners at Barkerville, the Chinese, or Celestials as they were called, were an enigma. They were as different as night from day, and while other minorities, notably the Negroes, assimilated well into the community, the Chinese lived in a world of their own. They probably had to, for to his shame, the white man had no use for them. In newspaper accounts we often read of explosions where nobody was killed "except a couple of Chinamen", and a Chinese could be murdered for his gold poke, and a few questions might be asked, but nothing would ever come of it.

They seemed to have two passions; gambling and fighting amongst themselves, if the pages of the *Cariboo Sentinel* are to be believed. There were opium dens in which imported and Victoria-produced opium was smoked, and there was a "hospital" to which old men would come to die. Today, this building is known as Trapper Dan's cabin, named after Chin Fong, better known as Trapper Dan because of his unique occupation, as few Chinese operated trap lines. Trapper Dan died in Kamloops during the 1950s.

We will never know how many Chinese lived in Barkerville, as no records have survived, if indeed, they were kept. Estimates have placed the figure as high as 8000, and it is said there were eight restaurants catering to the Oriental trade here.

Life in the community evolved around the Chinese Freemasons, whose first Temple was opened in 1862—the first in what is now Canada—but was destroyed in the great fire of 1868. It was all things to all Chinamen, as nearly all belonged to it.

Chinese Masonic Hall

The Lodge served as a court to settle disputes, an employment bureau, community centre, funeral home, and medical clinic.

The present building bears three signs around the door. The top one gives the name of the lodge in Chinese characters, but the ones along the side are much more complex. They are Chinese poems, carefully worded, so that each character proves an opposite to its counterpart in the other poem. On the left-hand side of the building, the characters read "looking in front is my mountain range with its green tops." On the other side, the poem refers to the fact that "inside Buddha sits dignified." As can be seen, this cannot be translated into English and still retain the sense the Chinese scholars intended it to contain.

Inside the building was a picture of The Buddha, and at the ornate rail before it, incense was burned.

(The Chinese Freemasons are in no way connected with the A.F. & A.M. rites, being an independent order, going far back into Chinese history.)

A cemetery was set aside for the Chinese, close to the Roman Catholic one at Richfield and the first body was placed there in July 1866. Following the usual custom, the bones were gathered together at intervals and shipped back to China, but six graves with headboards still remain.

The Chinese working the mines were, for the most part, freemen, who had come up from Montana and California with the hordes of white miners. A few were indentured, but not many. The status of some women in the community might best be judged from this item which appeared in the *Sentinel* for August 10, 1872:

"SALE OF CELESTIAL TREASURE — We understand that a Celestial lady from the Flowery Kingdom changed hands during the week in Barkerville at the handsome figure of $700. It is said that the lady, who is a votary of the Cyprian goddess, feels highly elated that her entrancing charms and wonderful fascinations should have realized such a satisfactory price. We recommend the subject to the consideration of the Grand Jury at the next Assizes. That young ladies from the Celestial Empire should be bartered and sold under their very eyes ought to be productive of the most intense indignation in the breast of every Grand Juror who is imbued with a British horror of slavery and a love of freedom."

We do not know what the Chinese section looked like in the early days, and the only published account we seem to have is an unflattering one

Opium Equipment

Exhibit Cabin, Chinatown

which appeared in the *Sentinel* for August 7, 1869:—

"Chinatown is universally voted a nuisance in Barkerville in every shape, sense or manner. Pigs are fed in the streets in front of the buildings; there is no regular sidewalk, the drainage is corrupted with animal and every kind of filth; in short every inconvenience and disagreeableness characteristic of a semi-barbarous race is present in Chinatown. Let the Grand Jury take this subject into consideration with a view to removing or modifying these evils. Pig-feeding in the streets ought to be stopped forthwith. A great many Chinamen have been sick lately, and no wonder. Let us compel them, however, for our own safety, to pay some attention to sanitary conditions. We have now a neat, clean-looking town, but its neatness is marred by the causes above referred to."

On the hill beside Chinatown can be seen the terraces which the patient Chinese made on which to grow vegetables.

The Chinese—who laboured hard for their gold—have now deserted the creeks. Their "last stand" was at Slough Creek, near the Ketch mine, where, during the thirties, four companies, known as the Quong Lee, Sing Dang, Dang Sing Dang and Loo Gee Wing worked the benches by the hydraulic process, and it is estimated recovery was as high as $300,000.

Since the early days, a great change has taken place in the relations between the Oriental and the Occidental, and today the two live side by side, with the Chinese often playing a leading role in the community.

BARKERVILLE'S CHURCHES

OF ALL THE CHURCHES which stood in Barkerville and Richfield—Roman Catholic, Wesleyan, Presbyterian and Welsh, only St. Saviour's Anglican remains.

The story of its beginnings is a tale of hardship and devotion, neither more nor less than that experienced by the other denominations, who, as the Rev. James Reynard, a one-time rector of St. Saviour's wrote in the *Sentinel*, the task was to provide "a church which shall prove that men working underground have still some hopes which go upward and heavenward."

During construction of the church, the *Sentinel* said:

"The new church now building promises to be an elegant structure. It is built from designs by the Rev. J. Reynard, which are being ably carried out by Messrs. Bruce & Mann. The style is 'Early English' in which architectural effect is attained by due proportion of parts, bold and simple forms, rather than by elaborate ornament. The church will consist of— nave, 30 ft. x 20 ft., and apsidal chancel, 16 ft. x 12 ft. Height of walls, 18 feet; of ceiling, from floor, 23 feet. A schoolroom and vestry complete the building. We congratulate the friends of the Anglican Church on possessing a church so appropriate to their worship. Certainly those who wish to pray, as their fathers prayed, may do so here, in a church which in form, if not in material, will remind them of the village churches of the "fatherland."

The Rev. James M. Reynard was not the first Anglican missionary on the Creek. Before him had been Rev. R. Lundin Brown, who had tried to "clean-up" the gamblers in Cameronton without meeting too much success, and the Rev. C. Knipe, both of whom were there during 1861. They were followed by the Rev. John Sheepshanks and the Rev. R. J. Dundas, who also visited Van Winkle, Antler and Cottonwood.

In 1863 a site was chosen for a "small, substantial, well-proportioned building" to be erected at a cost of $1200. Sheepshanks took in a library of about 250 books, but this church was never built as the mission fell vacant for two years until Reynard, a former Methodist minister from Yorkshire arrived to take up the work.

A former saloon was purchased for use as a church on Sundays and a school during the weekdays, but within two weeks after his arrival, the great fire wiped out his work.

"All my efforts and expenditures have been in vain," he wrote, "the Institute obliterated, all my lamps, benches, robes and books are gone without a trace. The old church at Barkerville, by the sale of which I had hoped to pay for the labor of building our new cottage, is gone, and which way to turn I know not. I have no church, save that at Richfield, and that has not yet been glazed, and there is not a pane of glass in the place. . . .

St. Saviour's Anglican Church

Most people advise me to "leave at once" but this I cannot do, dare not, will not think of."

That winter was one of great hardship for Reynard, and in another letter he states:

"We live as cheaply as possible; Potatoes on Sundays by way of marking the Christian feast and cabbage on Christmas as a very special luxury. We tried more stringent economies than these but I was losing my memory and getting morbidly afraid of meeting people. . . ."

During this period he remarked that he had great difficulty in keeping the Tenth Commandment when he heard the bell of the Roman Catholic Church at Richfield, which had been dedicated by Bishop d'Herbomez two weeks before his arrival.

Every cent he could muster together was put into the building fund, including a large share of his small stipend, but "the people of Barkerville now grieved me much", for support from them was not forthcoming.

Months went by, and finally, some of the leading merchants came to his assistance, and on Sunday, September 24, 1870, he was able to hold his first services in the new church. A year later, Reynard moved to Nanaimo, and in 1875 he died at Saanich, still a young man; the rigours of the Cariboo had claimed another victim.

A similar pattern of hardship was shown by all "men of the cloth" who came to the gold camps of the Cariboo.

The first Roman Catholic priest to visit Williams Creek came in 1861, but it was not until 1868 that St. Patrick's Church was erected at Richfield.

The Wesleyan Methodists came in 1863, but it was not until June 20, 1869 that the Rev. Thomas Derrick was able to have his church dedicated.

The first and only Presbyterian minister in the Cariboo before Confederation was the Rev. D. Duff, who stayed on the creek for 13 months holding morning services at Cameronton and evening ones at Richfield.

In 1866 the Welsh group built the Cambrian Hall for "literary religious purposes". Services were conducted by John Evans. It was destroyed by the fire, and rebuilt, but the mines had become less rich and no great success was achieved by the Cambrian Society after the fire.

63

Pack train and cattle drive in old Barkerville

BOWRON HOUSE

ONE OF THE MOST respected names in Barkerville, from 1862 onwards, was that of "Bowron" and in the historic park, this name is represented in the Bowron House, built in 1898 by William Bowron.

Across the road can be seen the stumps of the row of trees which once graced the home of his father, John Bowron, the librarian at Cameronton and Barkerville, and later Gold Commissioner.

William Bowron was born in Barkerville on April 13, 1872 and lived here until about 1912. He died at Bella Coola in 1944.

The furniture inside the Bowron House consists of authentic period pieces, and perhaps the most interesting is the Kelly piano, being played by one of the papier-mache models created by Mrs. Herbert T. Cowan of North Vancouver. This piano is said to have been brought in on the backs

The Bowron House

of six human packers in the 1860s for one of the saloons of Barkerville. The great book on the table is the Bowron family Bible.

John Bowron was a member of the famous "Overlanders of '62", who believed that the route across the prairies and through the Yellowhead Pass was the "easy" way to get to the Cariboo. It did not take long for them to get disillusioned. In 1866 he was appointed postmaster at Williams Creek, succeeding J. R. Commeline who left the Cariboo and went to Australia to take a government job in Brisbane.

He had studied law back in Cleveland, Ohio, with his brother-in-law, and this stood him in good stead at Williams Creek, where, in 1872 he was appointed to the important post of Mining Recorder. Three years later, he was Government Agent, and in 1883 was given the position of Gold Commissioner, working out of the office which today, like the home of his son, is a "museum piece." Bowron retired in 1906 and died in September of the same year.

Interior, Bowron House

THE CEMETERY

THE OLD BARKERVILLE, or Cameronton Cemetery, high on a bench overlooking the spot where John A. "Cariboo" Cameron struck it rich, is like a story book written on wooden and marble headmarkers.

Here lie the argonauts, both men and women. They came from Canada, the United States, Cornwall, Ireland, Wales, the Lake Country of England, Scotland, France, Russia, Mexico and other lands. Most of them died young: some through rheumatism caused by working long hard hours in icy cold water and then having no fresh, dry clothes to change into; some fell down shafts, and others were stricken with typhoid or mountain fever.

The site was chosen by Cameron himself, and with his foreman, James Cummings, he cleared the land, and the first to be placed in it was Peter Gibson of Vankleekhill, Canada West, who died of mountain fever on July 24, 1863 at the age of 31.

The sign at the entrance to the Cemetery is one of the most interesting in Barkerville, reading:

" 'One of Cariboo Cameron's men died and they hauled him up the side hill and planted him there!'

Fred Tregillus.

"And so this historic cemetery came into being with burial of Peter Gibson, 31 years of age, on July 24, 1863.

"The great and the not-so-great from the gold rush era lie in this peaceful setting.

"Please respect these consecrated acres with their time-honoured tributes to those that forever have a place in Barkerville."

The following is a list of some of the more interesting headstones, in alphabetical order, and stories about them:

ALLEN, Janet; Sacred to the memory of—Beloved wife of William Allen. Native of Fifeshire, Scotland. Who Departed this life Sept. 4 1870. Aged 42. "Scotch Jenny" as she was known lies buried behind a picket fence, and two great balsam trees nearly obscure the wooden headboard. While driving over to Williams Creek from her saloon at Dunbar Flats on Lightning Creek, she turned to speak to a miner walking behind the buggy, and accidentally pulled too much on one rein, forcing the buggy over the bank. Jenny broke her neck in the fall. Said the Sentinel: "Mrs. Allen came to Cariboo in 1862 and acquired the respect of everyone by the numerous acts of kindness she performed in cases of sickness or distress. Whenever any accident occurred or any case of serious illness she volunteered her services to become nurse and friend of the miner. She exhibited this humane disposition at considerable inconvenience to herself. . . . All the flags in Barkerville were hung at half mast."

BENNETT, James. In memory of, A native of the parish of Pont i hyr v

67

Fryn, Glanmorganshire, Wales, who died August 1, 1868, aged 37. (The Welsh inscription is indecipherable.) Bennett was killed in the Taffvale claim on Stouts Gulch when a cave-in occurred. Bancroft says this claim had five shafts, all of which were "lost" before the drainage used by the mines below were extended to its boundaries. It cost $30,000 to open and yielded finally from 100 to 200 ounces of gold per week.

The *Sentinel* noted in his obituary that he had just quit his job at the claim and was working his last shift.

BILSLAND, John, *In memoryy of, Died Mach (sic) 13, 1879. Aged 43.* Killed by a snowslide from the roof of the shaft house of the Two Brothers Claim, Jack of Clubs Creek. He was "greatly respected" noted the Victoria *Colonist* and between 250 and 300 miners attended the funeral.

BLAIR, James. *At Rest. Died March 26, 1885. Aged 35.* Killed in a cave-in on the Mason Claim on Antler Creek.

BLAIR, Margaret Jane. *In memory of, Beloved wife of John Pinkerton. Died May 30, 1880, aged 21 years 7 mos. Also their daughter, died April 19, 1879, aged 10 days.*

> *O cruel death; thou waster severe*
> *To snatch so suddenly away*
> *This cherished loved-one in her prime*
> *To mix among the moudering clay.*

A tiny tombstone next to it reads *MJP*.

BLYTHE, John. *To the memory of, Native of Fifeshire, Scotland. Aged 47.* Date of death indecipherable.

BOVYER, Jas. R., *in memory of, of Charlotte Town, Prince Edward Island. Died 31st Janry 1870. Aged 32.* While working near Mosquito Creek in 1867 he was cut severely in the back part of the head by accidentally falling on an axe. "We understand," reported the *Sentinel,* "he died of congestion of the brain."

BOWRON, Archie Ray. *Beloved son of John and Emily Bowron. Died 30 Oct. 1889, aged 7 months. Our Darling.*

BOWRON, Emily. *Beloved wife of John Bowron GC. Born at Clifton Michigan, April 25, 1850. Died at Barkerville May 29, 1895.* The wife of the gold commissioner she was married at Richfield August 16, 1869. She had two other sons, besides Archie Ray, Eddie and William (see page 65) and two daughters, Alice and Lottie. Following her death, John Bowron married an Elizabeth Watson.

BREW, Chartres. *In memory of, Born at Corsfin, County Clare Ireland. 31 Dec. 1815. Died at Richfield, 31 May 1870. Gold Commissioner and County Court Judge. A man impertureable in courage and temper endowed with a great & varied administrative capacity. A most ready wit a most pure integrity.* It is said these words were written by his friend Judge Matthew Baillie Begbie. Prior to coming to British Columbia late in 1858 he served with the Irish Constabulary in Cork, and during the summer of 1858 was offered the appointment of Chief Commissioner of Police by the colonial secretary Sir Edward B. Lytton. Soon after his arrival he was sent to Yale to aid handling a disturbance of the miners there and was made chief Gold Commissioner. In the summer of 1859 he returned to Victoria and soon afterwards was appointed stipendiary magistrate at New Westminster. In 1867 he went to Cariboo. In 1864 Brew commanded a party of New Westminster volunteers against the Chilcotin Indians following the murder of the Waddington survey party, and for this service he received from the Colonial government a service of plate in acknowledgement of his services.

"As the magistrate and gold commissioner of the Cariboo," noted the *Sentinel*, "Mr. Brew secured the esteem and respect of the whole community by his impartiality and manifest intentions to do justice in matters brought before him. As an individual he displayed much interest in the natural productions and resources of the colony, collecting specimens and bringing them into the notice, encouraging scientific research and in so doing showed that he possessed a large stock of useful and general knowledge. The position he held here is a difficult one to fill, all matters relating to gold mining bearing so much complexity . . . yet he managed to discharge his duties in the most creditable manner to the general satisfaction of the inhabitants of Cariboo."

In 1835 he had served under Sir DeLacy Evans in the Spanish Legion and was severely wounded. On his return home he entered the Irish Constabulary, and on the outbreak of the Crimean War he was appointed Deputy Assistant Commissary General, later becoming Assistant Commissary General.

BROWN, Bill. In memory of. Born near Westport, Ontario, Dec. 16, 1839. Died January 19, 1939. Brown came to Barkerville in 1872, and Bruce Hutchison in his *The Fraser* states: "An ancient man with a Santa Claus beard was sitting by the belly of the drum stove (in the Kelly Hotel) when I came in. He looked up at me suspiciously. His name was Bill Brown, he was one of the Argonauts, he lived alone in the hills and came to town for a bit of excitement now and then. But he would not talk to strangers. This turned out to be a big night in Barkerville, for three other outsiders drove in my automobile—too big a night for Bill Brown. At the sight of this mass invasion he shuffled out of the hotel without a word, mounted his horse almost as old as himself, and rode out of town."

CAMERON, John A. In loving memory of. Died Nov. 7, 1888. Aged 68 years. A native of Glengarry, Ontario. See page 10.

CASTAGNETTE, F. In memory of, native of Rappalo, Italy. Died July 4, 1882. Aged 44. At Rest. "For many years," said the Victoria *Colonist,* "he was very prosperous and in 1868 was a wealthy merchant in Barkerville, and one of the heaviest losers in the fire." After the fire he went to Nevada and California.

"The funeral was held in the Theatre Royal, the Methodist church being too small. . . . The deceased was an upright man of singularly amiable disposition and his early death is greatly deplored."

CRAWFORD, W. J., In memory of, of Port Hope, C.W. Died July 23, 1864. Aged about 30 years.

DAOUST, Felix, Sacred to the memory of, native of (indecipherable) Quebec. Died at Barkerville 8th of August 1872. Rest in Peace. His name frequently appears in Masonic notices in the *Sentinel.*

DENNY, Joseph. September 5, 1891. He was a saloonkeeper, and in the Sept. 24, 1870 issue of the *Sentinel* it is noted that in partnership with Charles House, he had taken over the St. George's Saloon.

DOW, George Alfred, In loving memory of, beloved husband of Fanny Dow. Born at Walsea Island, Essex, England May 5, 1842. Died at Barkerville B.C. Jan. 2nd 1902. Asleep in Jesus.

DUNN, John, Sacred to the memory of, native of Wick, Glanmorganshire, South Wales, who died at 1 o'clock a.m., Oct. 6, 1863. Aged 24 years. Nghanoel ein bywyd yr ydym mewm angau. A direct translation of this Welsh phrase is *In the midst of our life we are in sorrow* or more freely *In the midst of life we are in death* which is taken from an antiphon written in 912 AD by the monk Notker as he was watching construction of a bridge at Martinstobel and saw the peril of the workers. It was usually sung before or after Nunc Dimittis. Dunn apparently was one of a large body of Welsh miners who came to the Cariboo to work in the mines where the experience gained in the coal mines back home stood them in good stead.

EASTER, Donald, *Sacred to the memory of. 21 Sept. 1864. Aged 29 years.*

EDWARDS, Rosser, *In memory of, native of Tredegar, Monmouthshire, South Wales, who died 29 Nov. 1867, aged 45 years.* Edwards was drowned in a mineshaft. He helped to take Sophia Cameron's body from Williams Creek to Keithley Creek.

ENERSON, Ener, *In loving memory of. Died Feb. 15, 1903. Age 38 years.*

FRANKLYN, Julius H., *In memory of, of the Island of Jersey. Died June 13, 1870. Aged 23 years.* He fell down a shaft at the Perserverance Company's claim on Mink Gulch, Harvey Creek, and was killed. He came to Victoria in 1862 and in 1864 went to Cariboo. Said the *Sentinel*: "At the request of the Jewish residents the Rev. Mr. Derrick (Rev. Thomas Derrick, Wesleyan) attended the funeral and the service at the grave consisted in the readings of portions from the Old Testament and an address suitable to the sudden death and afflictive occasion."

FRASER, J. A., *Sacred to the memory of, late of St. Andrew's C.W. Died 20 May 1865. Aged 32 years. May his soul rest in peace.* A civil engineer, John Alexander Fraser was the fourth son of Simon Fraser, the great explorer for the North West Company of Montreal, who followed the river which now bears his name from Fort George, now Prince George, to its mouth in 1808. Simon Fraser died in 1862. J. A. Fraser, who inherited his father's property, came to B.C. in 1864 and set himself up

as an engineer in Cameronton. To raise the money to come out west he mortgaged the property back at St. Andrew's and, although he apparently did well, he neglected to keep up the mortgage payments, and the place was foreclosed on him. This, plus an unhappy love affair, prompted him to commit suicide. The *Sentinel* noted, "His upright and generous disposition had secured him the esteem of all who knew him." Describing the funeral, the New Westminster *British Columbian* stated, "His remains were borne to their last resting place by his Masonic brethern and by the largest concourse of friends ever before assembled in Cariboo for such a purpose."

GIBSON, Peter, Sacred to the memory of, of Vankleekhill, County of Prescott, Canada West, who died July 24, 1863, Aged 31. See the introduction to this chapter. Under Robert Stevenson, Cariboo Cameron's partner, he had been a constable in the Osoyoos district before coming to Cariboo.

GILES, William, Sacred to the memory of, native of Missouri, U.S. Died May 3, 1869. Aged 36 years. According to the Victoria *Colonist* he came to B.C. in 1858 and was "familiarly known as Jack of Clubs and the discoverer of the creek so named." The lake took its name from the creek.

HAGEMAN, Marie, In memory of. Died July 23, 1888. Aged 59. Native of Germany. Rest in Peace.

HALL, Westley. May 1870. (?)

Jack of Clubs Lake, named after William Giles

HANSEN, Andrew, In memory of, native of Sweden. Born in the year of our Lord ____ . Died in the R.C. (Royal Cariboo) Hospital the 10th of October, 1883 from the effect of a fall in a shaft by which he broke his back and died afterward within six hours. What I say unto you I say unto all the world. If therefore thou shalt not watch, I will come on thee as a thief, and thou shalt not know what hour I will come upon thee. Apparently somebody did not want the rest of the world to know the birthdate of Andrew Hansen, or possibly there was an error in it, as the date has been neatly cut out of this strange headboard.

HILL, William W., In memory of, native of Nottingham, England. Died 23 Oct. 1896. Aged 37. The Sentinel says, "He was a very intelligent and amiable man and had gained a large number of friends in Cariboo." Hill left England in 1857 for Canada where he prospered quite well as a "painter" and came to B.C. in 1863. He was a member of the amateur dramatic group and the William Creek Fire Brigade. For a year prior to his death he had been in poor health and was on his way to Williams Lake "for a change of air" when he died at Cottonwood. "The Fire Brigade turned out in uniform and followed the funeral procession. A large number of citizens also attended."

HITCHCOCK, William, Sacred to the memory of, late government assayer, Barkerville, Cariboo. Born in London, Eng., Jan. 15, 1824. Departed this life Sept. 9, 1877. May he rest in peace. Hitchcock was in government service for 18 years, eight of which he spent in the Cariboo. Prior to coming to Barkerville he was Assistant Refiner at the B.C. Government Mint at New Westminster. He served as a member of New Westminster City Council, elected for Ward 4, on April 19, 1866.

HODGKINSON, Isabella, IHS, In loving memory of, aged 66 years. Died Oct. 5, 1911. Sleep, Bella, Sleep. In God We Trust. Bella Hodgkinson supported herself, and sometimes her husband, Billy, by taking in washing. It was her proud boast that she was the earliest riser in the Williams Creek camp or any of its tributaries. Few disputed her or tried to compete, least of all her husband. "Why don't you sleep," he would plead to her, for the rattle of boilers and tubs disturbed his rest. But Bella,

who had her reputation to maintain, wouldn't listen. And so, wrote Louis LeBourdais "when the call came and the rattle of boilers and tubs had ceased and they laid her away, Bill Hodgkinson, in his grief, had the words "Sleep, Bella, Sleep. In God we trust" written on her tombstone. Billy is also buried in the cemetery but the final resting place is not known.

HOUSE, *Charles Wesley, native of Syracuse, New York. Born August 3, 1834. Died May 22, 1913. At Rest.*
With Joseph Denny, who is also buried here, he purchased the St. George's Saloon in September 1870. He was known as the "Beau Brummel of Williams Creek". Husband of Margaret House, see below.
HOUSE, *Margaret, Sacred to the memory of, born Germany, May 30, 1854. Died Dec. 12, 1939. At Rest.* Mrs. House came to Barkerville as a young girl in 1875, with her sister the late Mrs. (Jeanette) Housser, who died in 1933. For 55 years she lived in the House Hotel. She made one trip "outside" and that was in the summer of 1876 when she returned to San Francisco to bring back her five-year-old nephew, Willie Housser, who had been left behind when the Houssers came to B.C. in 1875. Mrs. House, then Margaret Ceise, made the 3,000 mile trip by stage coach and steamer. On her return trip she was met at Soda Creek by Charles House who had wooed and won her before she left for San Francisco. They were married a few days later at Barkerville, and for 50 years after her marriage she ventured no further away than Wingdam, 30 miles westward. A few years before she died she went as far as Quesnel.
HOUSE, *Wesley Charles, In memory of. Died August 4, 1917. Age 33 years.*
HOUSSER, *Jeanette, In loving memory of, 1840-1933. Mother.* See Margaret House.
HOUSSER, *Edward, In memory of. Died June 16, 1926. Age 41.*
HUGILL, *William, In memory of, late of Fullerton, Canada West, who died Aug. 31, 1863, aged 25. Blessed are the pure in heart, for they shall see God. Inscribed as a token of ESTEEM by his Overland companions.* Hugill was one of several parties who came from Canada *via* the so-called "easy route to Cariboo", across the prairies and through the Yellowhead Pass in 1862. He lies next to Peter Gibson, the first to be buried in the Cameronton cemetery.
JOHNSTON, *George, In memory of, native of Colchester County, N.S. Died May 7, 1865, aged 36 years.* The Victoria *Colonist* stated he "died on Lowhee Creek of a disease, called by Dr. Brown who attended him, the 'gum-boot gout'."
JONES, *Wm. Ll., a native of Beaufort, Wales. Born July 5, 1836. Died August 18, 1888.*
KELLY, *Alexander. Born March 24, 1878. Died March 26, 1878.*
KELLY, *Johnny Hastie, born at Grouse Creek, June 1, 1869. Died March 10, 1875.*
KELLY, *James A., In loving memory of. Died at Barkerville, April 3, 1894.*
KIMBALL, *E. H., Sacred to the memory of, native of Bradford, Mass. Died the 31st of January 1874. Aged 38 years.* The Keithley Creek expressman, he was killed by an avalanche near the gorge of Six Mile Creek. "It appears," noted the Victoria *Colonist*, "that he was in company

with Kansas John. . . . Besides the mail and the express, it is said, he had a considerable treasure in his possession at the time of the accident. . . . He was a very well educated man and was highly esteemed by all who knew him." Some 48 hours after the accident the body was recovered with the treasure and express strapped to him.

LEWIS, *Griffith, In memory of, native of Pulleg, Breconshire, South Wales, who died 12 April 1867, aged 31 years.* The *Sentinel* noted he "died of inflammation of the bowels" and that he "was worth several thousand dollars which he made in Cariboo." Lewis died in the Royal Cariboo Hospital.

LYNCH, *Mathew, In memory of, 20 July 1874. Aged 42 years.* According to the Victoria *Colonist* Lynch was "steady and industrious". A miner, working on the Russell - Robinson Co. claim on Lowhee Creek, he was found dead on the Lowhee Trail near the Black Bull Co.'s claim. He had visited the store at Richfield, but the wind had drifted the snow over the trail and he became lost. Exhausted by his wandering about, Lynch died about half a mile from his cabin. The *Colonist* said he was "a natural-ized American, but an Irishman by birth."

LINDSAY, *James. Late Quarter Mr. Sergeant Royal Artillery. Died Feb. 17, 1890, aged 82. May his soul rest in peace.* William V. Bowron, in a typescript *"Impressions of Barkerville"* deposited in the Provincial Archives in Victoria has this to say of Q.M.S. Lindsay. He was "better known as Whispering Jimmie. He used to indulge to quite an extent in 'Old Barleycorn' and when under the influence, always had some secret to impart and would take one aside to whisper it, but as his whisper was more penetrating than his ordinary tone of voice, his secrets always became public property. When I first became aware of his position in society I was greatly impressed with his importance and later on, after seeing him make a few arrests, was in deadly terror of him and whenever he came to the house, which he did almost daily, I would conceal myself and if by chance he should come on me unawares, was usually nice and polite to him. The only arrests he ever made (that I can remember) were for drunkenness and when this occurred he would probably be more under the influence than the arrestee. . . ." Lindsay was the constable and jailer at Richfield in the 1870s, and it is said he seldom ever locked the jail door. In 1875 he was Registrar of the County Court at Richfield.

McINTYRE, *Archibald. In loving memory of, born at Lochaweside, Scotland. Died at Barkerville 20th April 1906, aged 49 years. A faithful friend and a true-hearted Highlander. Erected by his sorrowing sister Kilchrenan. Ever so dear brother, until the grey shadows fall and the day eternal dawns, they shall behold the land that is very far off. S fhada an gladeth bho lochodha.* McIntyre was a partner with George Clarke in a sawmill on the site of present-day Wells. This stone was probably sent out from Scotland by his sister; the Gaelic can be translated as "long have been kept from home" and is in all likelihood a line from some Gaelic poetry.

McIntyre's birthplace, Lochaweside, is near Oban, and it is interesting to note that the neighbouring village has the same name as his sister, Kilchrenan.

McKENNA, Patrick. *In memory of, native of Duleck, County Meath, Ireland. Died June 2, 1914. Aged 59. R.I.P.* A former Chicago policeman, who with Abe Stott, who is buried in the Stanley cemetery, discovered gold at Eight Mile Creek while on a fishing trip. Mining men and old timers alike maintained there could be no gold there.

McKINNON, Lottie Mabel, *August 15, 1883 - March 27, 1956.* A native of Barkerville, Mrs. McKinnon spent her entire life in the community. Her father was Henry Brown and her first husband was William Kelly who operated the Kelly Hotel and store. In 1919 she married Malcolm McKinnon. For years she managed the hotel and store and directed the operations of a transportation and contracting business. When she died the *Cariboo Observer* of Quesnel said "Prospectors were grubstaked during the lean years and other ventures received her backing. Her husband, Malcolm McKinnon, came to Cariboo in 1906 and died May 21, 1943, aged 67.

McLAREN, John. *Sacred to the memory of, of Williams Town, Coy of Glengarry, Canada. Died Aug. 7, 1869. Aged 31 years. Friends must part. Erected by his Cariboo friends as a token of their esteem.* Before coming out to B.C. in 1864 he had been headmaster of Williamstown

Royal Cariboo Hospital, 1896, which stood just below cemetery

County Grammar School, whose student body, according to the Cornwall *Freeholder* "take this opportunity of collectively expressing their deep sorrow at his untimely end, that they testify with a melancholy pleasure to his fine mental powers and goodness of heart." The school and the students set up a memorial scholarship in his memory. During the winter of 1866-67 he was editor of the *Cariboo Sentinel*. The paper reported he had been covered with sand and tailings at the Columbia Shaft on Williams Creek. At the inquest, two cousins, Alex A. Robertson and James Dingwall testified. Robertson said the estate consisted of $15, ten of which he had in his pocket when killed. "His numerous friends," continued the *Sentinel*, "contemplate erecting a marble monument to commemorate his death and their grief at his loss."

McLEAN, J. L. B. *In memory of. (colored) at Richfield. Died February 4, 1911. Aged 75 years.* Miss Lottie Bowron remembers McLean as being the caretaker at the Court House at Richfield when her father, John Bowron, was Gold Commissioner and had the office moved down to Barkerville. Johnny McLean got $5 a month for doing this work.

McLURE, Thomas (?) *April 1873 (?)..*

McQUEEN, Duncan. *In memory of, native of Halifax, Nova Scotia. Died 21 June 1866. Aged 38.*

MALANION, J. B. *In memory of, Born in France. Died Feb. 1, 1879. Aged 55 years.* Malanion was a violinist and had played with the Paris Opera and in Barkerville taught music, but his main livelihood came from his being a carpenter. John McLean, a hotel keeper at Quesnel at a later date, told this story of Malanion's death: When he was dying in the old Cariboo Hospital, in a bed next to his lay O. G. Travaillot, also dying. Both knew they could not survive the night, so true to the last to the spirit of the camp, they wagered fifty cents as to who would die first. Toward morning Malanion's voice rang out clear as a bell: "Captain Travaillot, you win. I lose. I die now." His head dropped as his voice rang out.

MASON, Joseph. *In loving memory of, died Dec. 2, 1890, aged 51 years.* An Englishman, Mason came to Barkerville in 1866, and in the *Sentinel* for Aug. 7, 1869 it is recorded that with J. Daley he was keeper of the Antelope Restaurant. Later he was a general merchant with many mining interests, and writing in 1930, Louis LeBourdais said "people in Barkerville still date events by the death of Joe Mason."

MITCHELL, Wm. L. *In memory of, of St. Mary's, C.W. Died 24 May 1867. Aged 32.* William Lang Mitchell was killed while being lowered down the Davis Co. shaft, falling 36 feet and landing on his head. The *Sentinel* noted that he was "one of the proprietors of the *British Colonist* and more recently as part proprietor of the *Evening Express and Telegraph*, Victoria." After closing up his Victoria business he bought a half share in the Davis claim "and arrived here about a month ago." The accident occurred after he had been on the job for only two weeks. "On Saturday," said the *Sentinel*, "the flags in town were raised to half mast

Barkerville Old Timers

out of respect to the deceased. . . . In the absence of a clergyman the English funeral was read by Mr. Robertson, barrister, and many were affected. . . ."

MITTON, James H. Died Dec. 1867. This headstone is indecipherable.

MONTGOMERY, Samuel. Born Oct. 28, 1814, Enniskillen, Fermanagh, Ireland. June 1, 1904. Sam Montgomery was one of the most colourful characters in the Cariboo, and the late Harry Jones MLA (see Stanley cemetery), in a series of articles with Louis LeBourdais which appeared in The Vancouver Province in April 1935 recalled at length the story of Sam.

"Sam Montgomery had been a sailor for many years before he struck Cariboo in '62; had a captain's certificate, but used to say that he preferred the companionship of the men in the fo'c'stle and invariably shipped as an able seaman. When he was "half seas over" he would sometimes tell us of his experiences. At other times, however, he had very little to say of the sea.

"He must have caught the gold fever from the '49ers, for his vessel had called at different California ports as early as 1847. He was aboard the Blackball liner Caleb Grimshaw when that vessel took fire at sea some time in the 1840s, I think it was. Only after he had been an a fairly legendary spree would he speak of the harrowing incidents which occurred; but from snatches of his conversation on these occasions, we gathered that the tragedy must have been terrible indeed. Passengers and crew totalled more than three hundred souls; some had gone stark mad and many jumped overboard, upsetting liferafts and boats. The fire had been battened down but the ship got so hot that the men were finally forced to climb into the rigging. The water supply became exhausted and for days the only moisture available was whiskey, and with this the poor thirst-crazed wretches moistened their lips to prevent them from cracking open. The few survivors were eventually rescued by a passing vessel.

"Sam was forty-two years in Cariboo, most of the time on Lightning and Nelson Creeks, without a single trip outside. Forty-two years of hard work with very little return in the way of comfort or luxury. . . . At the age of 82 Sam staked a claim on part of the old Van Winkle ground, which was abandoned, sunk a shaft to a depth of fifty-three feet, and then ran a seventy-eight foot drift. He handled and hoisted every bucketfull of dirt in the entire operation. He found course gold, but not in paying quantities.

"Montgomery partnered with us in one or two ventures in which he made a little stake, but unfortunately, the money did him little good. The 'Little Van Winkle' commonly known as the 'Montgomery Company' was his last strike, and no doubt hastened his end.

"In 1902 the Montgomery Company ran on to a piece of very rich ground which paid handsomely its five shareholders—Sam Montgomery, Fred Tregillus, George Rankin, Joe Spratt and myself [Harry Jones]. (Harry Eden was one of the originals, but he did not get along with fighting Joe Spratt and dropped out). The ground, which once belonged to the South Wales, paid as high as 100 ounces to a ten-foot cap.

"No books were kept. Enough gold was sold after each cleanup, which took place almost daily when the company was in good ground, to pay the wages. The rest was divided up equally, by weight, and any small balance thrown back in the common 'jackpot' for current expenses.

"Stanley was a lively place while the Montgomery was working and its consumption of playing cards, I once heard a commercial traveller declare, had any wide-open frontier town beaten that he had ever heard of. It was the custom in those days at least, for a man to throw his cards on the floor and call for a new deck if he was having a streak of bad luck. Usually, by morning, the floor would be literally carpeted with layers of brand new cards which had been tossed over the shoulders of disgruntled players. One single night's card bill at Len Ford's Hotel, I recall, totalled $77. And cards were cheap in those comparatively tax-free days.

"Toward the end of May 1904 Sam was taken to the hospital in Barkerville. He was then in his 90th year. On the morning of June 1, I called to see him. He asked me to stop in again on my way back to Stanley.

" 'I want you to get me out of this place,' he pleaded. 'I would like to do a little prospecting at the head of Jawbone Creek. John Fobiana told me he found good prospects there. And John would not say so unless it was true.'

"I promised to call, and I did. But the old prospector's spirit had proved to be stronger than the flesh. Sam's frail frame lay on the hospital bed; but his spirit had gone."

NORDBURG, T. W. *Sacred to the memory of, a native of Russia. Died Feb. 1, 1881. Aged 44 years.* During the 1870s he was a watchmaker, and in W. V. Bowron's *Impressions of Barkerville* in the Provincial Archives in Victoria, it is noted that Nordburg was "another queer character who did not disdain from the effects of Barleycorn. He was of a different type from the others, more of a recluse. One of his stunts was to act as chief mourner at Chinese funerals. He would parade up and down Chinatown making the most mournful sounds and weeping copiously. For this, it was said, he received the sum of five dollars and a skinful of booze, and one would think by his actions, that advance payment was always made in booze."

PARK, Joseph. *Sacred to the memory of, barrister-at-law. Native of Lancashire, England. Died 26 Jan. 1877. Aged 49 years.* According to Elliott's *Quesnel, Commercial Centre of the Cariboo Gold Rush,* he was an exceedingly clever lawyer, and one day while drunk fell into a flume between Barkerville and Richfield and died the next day.

PATTULLO, Thomas H. *a native of Ontario and an early pioneer of British Columbia. Born Dec. 16, 1837. Died Jan. 3, 1879.* A "before the fire" resident of Barkerville. In the April 6, 1872 issue of the *Sentinel* it is recorded that Mr. Pattullo raised $615 to permit a miner, stricken with an attack of consumption, to leave the Cariboo. The paper stated "too much praise cannot be given to Mr. Pattullo for his exertions in aid of the sick and needy. . . ." He is said to have taken an active part in organizing baseball in B.C., as early as 1864. He was an uncle of Thomas Duff Pattullo, premier of B.C. from 1933 to 1941.

PHILLIPS, William H. *In memory of, native of Gwiner, Cornwall, England. Aged 36 years. Died March 2, 1869.* The Victoria *Colonist* said a miner named Jesse Pierce had a fight with Phillips at Mosquito Gulch, and in the affray, Phillips received a kick in the abdomen which ruptured a vessel and died within a few hours. No charges were laid against Pierce, the paper added.

PINKERTON, Mathew. *At Rest. Died April 22, 1897. Aged 55.* Miss Lottie Bowron remembers him as a "well known cheery character" who was good to children. He was the brother of John Pinkerton, one of the Overland Party of '62, whose wife, Margaret Jane Blair, and daughter are buried in the Cameronton cemetery. Miss Bowron says, "Matt used to dance in mocassins, not much of a dancer I thought."

POND, George. *Sacred to the memory of, native of Roxborough, Mass. U.S. Died May 18, 1883. Aged 51 years.* He came to the Creek in 1862 and at the time of his death was a clerk for Mason and Daly.

RESTIDO, Harcosporis (?) Died July 19, 1880. Aged 9 months.
RODDICK, Ellie (1870 - 1948). John P. Roddick (1860 - 1948).
Mr. Roddick, a one-time foreman for the Lowhee interests, was born in
Meanbank, Scotland and came to Canada in the 1890s, settling in
Barkerville area around 1897. He predeceased his wife by 18 days. Mrs.
Roddick was born in Australia and came to Canada as a governess in
1898. Up until 1944 she was an active member of St. Saviour's Church
and played the organ there for 34 years.
ROGERS—In memory of, Dec. 19th, 1866. Aged 28.
ROGERS, S. A. In memory of, Our friend. God touched him and he
slept. June 4, 1911. Until the day breaks and the shadows fall away.
Song of Songs IV:6. Samuel Augustus Rogers was born in Northern
Ireland in 1840 and came with his parents to settle in Ontario in 1844.
He was educated in the County of Prince Edward. A member of one of
the famed Overland Parties of 1862 he was sheriff of the Cariboo - Lillooet
district for four years and was a director of the Royal Cariboo Hospital.
Elected to the Legislative Assembly of B.C. as a conservative in 1890, he
was returned at the general election of 1894. At the 1898 election he was
defeated, but gained election in 1900, to be defeated again in 1903.
Rogers was a general merchant whose store was the former Hudson's Bay
Co. establishment in Barkerville.
RUDDELL, Robt. In memory of, late of Halton Co., Ontario. Died 5
Dec. 1867. Aged 34 years. Killed in a snow slide on Grouse Creek.
SIMCOCK, Samuel. In memory of. Died June 10, 1907 aged 83 years.
A saloon keeper, he lived "on the tailings" near Jack of Clubs Lake, in
what is now Wells. Miss Lottie Bowron recalls him as having a long white
beard which made him look like Santa Claus.
STEVENSON, John Wesley. Sacred to the memory of, a native of
Westfield, New Brunswick. Died Nov. 18, 1873. Aged 26 years 6
months.
STEWART, William. Sacred to the memory of, a native of Scotland.
Died Aug. 1, 1884. Aged 56 years. Erected by his friends.
STOBO, Alexander. In memory of, native of West Boag, Scotland. Died
April 29, 1869. Aged 39 years. He was drowned on the Caledonian
Claim, along with a Chinese miner, when water broke into the shaft. The
Sentinel said: ". . . he was a man whose loss is mourned by all who have
been acquainted with him in the Cariboo where he had perseveringly
toiled for the last eight years, but though his name may not be handed
down to posterity on the tablets of fame his memory will be ever cherished
by the circle which had the privilege of calling him friend. Unassuming,
cheerful, industrious and generous, ever ready and anxious to assist a friend
to the utmost of his power, he has gone to his long home honoured and
lamented: and though no marble monument will mark his resting place in
the interior wilds of Cariboo, it may be some consolation to his aged
mother to hear of the honourable esteem in which her son was justly held."
Between 300 and 400 miners stopped work to attend the funeral which

was held in the Masonic Lodge Rooms and conducted by Rev. Thomas Derrick.

WALKER, George J. Born Barkerville Dec. 31, 1869. Died March 18, 1912. Son of a pioneer resident, he succeeded John Bowron as gold commissioner.

WATSON, Adam. In memory of. Died 10th Oct. 1880. Aged 56 years. A native of Greenock, Scotland. Died of heart disease at Richfield.

WEBSTER, Mary A. Sacred to the memory of, West Worthing, England. Died June 29, 1864. Aged 53. May her soul rest in peace. She was a resident of Cameronton.

WHITEFORD, David. Sacred to the memory of, who departed this life Nov. 10, 1866. Aged 33. Born at Kilwinning, County Ayr, Scotland. By his exemplary character he won the esteem and respect of many sincere friends. (Erected by his co-partners in the Reid Claim, Conklins Gulch.)

WILKINSON, J. B., M.D. born in Canada. Died Nov. 3, 1869, aged 35 years. Erected by his Cariboo friends, Nov. 1880. Dr. Wilkinson was born in Eglinton, York County, Ontario and came to B.C. as a miner during the early stages of the gold rush. He was one of the first to reach Rich Bar at Quesnel. Although he had given up the practice of medicine to seek his fortune in the goldfields, when he saw the suffering and need for medical care on Williams Creek he returned to his profession. He was Mrs. John A. "Cariboo" Cameron's physician. He died at Richfield "after a week's illness."

WINTRIP, Mary. Sacred to the memory of, beloved wife of Edward Wintrip, who departed this life Sept. 2, 1879. Born Northumberland.

> Here perfect bliss can ne'er be found
> The honest mind—
> Midst changing scenes and dying friends
> Be Thou my all in all.

Many who lie buried in Barkerville, or the Cameronton Cemetery have no known resting place. At the south end of the cemetery is the "new" section, wherein stands a flag pole marking the Field of Honour for veterans of two world wars.

Another cemetery in the Williams Creek area is at Richfield, a Roman Catholic one, which stands near the site of St. Patrick's Church. Two headboards here are readable.

FITZPATRICK, Patrick. In memory of, of County Cavan, Ireland, who departed this life on the 15th March, 1868, aged 32 years. Requiescat in pace.

MULARD, T. LeCi-lit, Born in France, Decease le—Avril, 1869. Age de 44 cns. The Sentinel states he died April 12th. Theophile Mulard, or Mullard as the death notice in the newspaper gives it, was a native of the Department of Seine et Oise and had been working on Nelson Creek when stricken with paralysis.

Theatre Royal with fire alarm on top

Barkerville before the fire

THE ROAD IN

THE SIXTY-FIVE-MILE "ROAD-IN" to Barkerville from Quesnel was the last link of the Cariboo Road to be completed. It was pushed through in 1865 and until recently, it twisted and turned as it always had, but then modern roadbuilding equipment moved in, and took the turns out. It used to be said, and the story may not be true, that it was quite a sport for passengers on the stage coaches to count the turns on the road, but unfortunately, it was like counting sheep on a sleepless night, for before long, the contestants in the game were sound asleep.

Leaving Quesnel, named after Jules Maurice Quesnel, one of Simon Fraser's companions on his epic trip down the river which bears his name, the first point of interest is Cottonwood House.

COTTONWOOD HOUSE: At one time, Cottonwood boasted several buildings, and was in fact, a small community. All that remains today is the quaint old stopping place, Cottonwood House, and the barns which make a beautiful setting for the photographer. The House was built in 1864 and was operated by the Boyd family until recent years. The records kept by John Boyd are a priceless record of "life on the trail" and are in the possession of the Cariboo Historical Society at Quesnel.

LIGHTNING CREEK: Flowing through Wingdam is Lightning Creek, which like Williams Creek of Barkerville, was a stream of gold. Discovered early in 1861 it fostered the booming towns of Stanley and Van Winkle, further east, settlements which rose and fell with the tides of miners, and today, only the shell of Stanley remains, while Van Winkle has completely vanished.

The creek was discovered by a group of miners, led by Bill Cunningham, who had had a particularly rough trip in from Antler Creek, and whenever things got really rugged, Cunningham used his favorite phrase, "Boys, this is lightning!" His companions decided to name the creek after this expression, but here one of the cruelest twists of history and mining occurred, for they found no gold. What must Cunningham and the others have thought when in July of the same year, Ned Campbell opened a rich

Lightning Creek, at Wingdam

claim 100 yards above Van Winkle Creek and a general rush ensued? For several years thereafter, there was a large production of gold from shallow, easily worked gravel on Last Chance, Van Winkle Creeks, and from bench gravel on Nason Point, Butcher Bench and Spruce Canyon.

The claims were then largely abandoned and it was not until ten years later that the richest ground in the creek was found and worked when the Montgomery Company (see Samuel Montgomery story on page 87) went to work.

Lightning Creek is a 24-mile long tributary to the Cottonwood.

Ruins of Beaver Pass House

BEAVER PASS HOUSE: A few yards from the present road, and hugging the old, can be seen the ruins of the Beaver Pass House, one of the important stopping places on the Cariboo Road. These Houses offered hospitality to the traveller and rest to the weary, plus good nourishing foods, and, of course, a little moisture to ease parched, dusty throats. The Beaver Pass House closed in the middle 1930s, and owing to neglect soon collapsed under the weight of snow during a particularly heavy winter.

STANLEY CEMETERY: On a bench, just before reaching the old town of Stanley can be seen the last resting places for many of the Argonauts of the Cariboo. Only a handful of graves are marked by headboards, and not all these are readable, but a visit is well worth while.

BEEDY, Josiah Crosby. Born in Pennsylvania, U.S. Died Van Winkle B.C. January 27, 1880. Beedy could be described as one of the pioneers of transportation in British Columbia. In 1871, with Francis Jones Barnard, of Barnard's Express, the famed BX, he tried an experiment of putting two of "R. W. Thompson's Patent Indian Rubber Tire Road Steamers" on the Cariboo Road. This grotesque piece of equipment, which resembled a steam roller, was fitted out to carry the mail and the express, but they certainly were not suited for the rough and winding Cariboo Road. On their first trip out of Yale they lumbered through the canyon, setting a new record for slowness, until they reached Jackass Mountain, and there, their careers came to a sorry end. They just couldn't puff their way up the steep grade.

Following this venture Beedy was a partner in the firm of Beedy & Townsend at the old Van Winkle Store, Lightning Creek which advertised in the *Sentinel* that "They keep on hand everything required in a mining camp."

In 1878 he became interested in a quartz property on Burns Mountain, a mile and a half south east of Stanley, and built a small quartz mill at Van Winkle.

EVANS, John. An undecipherable marker beside the grave of Harry Jones marks the final resting place of the leader of the Welsh Adventurers, who died in 1877.

The Evans Party was formed in July 1862 and about 300 applicants asked to go on the expedition, but the rumour got around that the climate was sub-zero, and there were scalping Indians prowling in the woods, and when it came down to actually signing up, only 26 put their names to the contract. The main party reached Victoria on June 11, 1863, although Evans had arrived two months before and had primed the Victoria residents as to what his men were going to do. One Victoria newspaper said "every man of the 26 was picked for a particular job" but as Harry Jones, the last survivor of the party, once said, the first he heard of that was when he read it in the paper.

On reaching Cariboo four and a half weeks after leaving New Westminster, they staked a number of claims, below what is now the Stanley cemetery.

Evans had had three years' experience in a slate quarry in Wales, but this was far different from the mining of Cariboo, and each day, to his embarrassment, things seemed to go wrong. It was not long before half the members of the company became discouraged and left, including his son Taliesin (see Harry Jones entry.)

Each man had a number, and of those who remained in the Colony only two others, Harry Jones and Robert F. Pritchard, the blacksmith, remained on Lightning Creek. William Jones (No. 9) was killed by a falling tree at Antler; William Owen (No. 12) was drowned in the Stikine River, William Griffith (No. 13) was killed in a coal mine near Bellingham, Wash., Edward Jones (No. 14) died at Kamloops, Daniel Parry, (No. 15) died at New Westminster, and John Jones, (No. 21) died at Soda Creek.

Evans was elected to the B.C. Legislature and died while holding office in 1877.

GREEP, John. Sacred to the memory of, Native of Devon, England. Departed this life April — 1877, aged 38 years. May he live with God.

JONES, Harry. Born Carnarvonshire, Wales, September 29, 1840. With the "Welsh Adventurers" arrived in B.C. June 1863. Last survivor of the famous Evans Party and one of the Cariboo's best-known and best-loved pioneers. Represented Cariboo in B.C. Legislature 1903 · 09. Died February 25, 1936. Buried at Stanley, B.C. See John Evans. In the Evans Party there were nine Joneses, and to make matters simple, Evans gave each member of the 27-man party a number. As it turned out, Jones' "stuck with him" for he was No. 8—or Henry VIII. With Taliesin Evans, son of "Captain" John Evans, he was the youngest in the party.

Stanley Cemetery

The younger Evans died in the 1920s, having left the Cariboo in 1867 to become associated with Samuel Williams in the San Francisco *Bulletin*, later becoming its managing editor. When the *Bulletin* was absorbed by the *Chronicle* he founded the Oakland *Tribune*. Jones returned to Wales in 1876, but ten years later, heard the call of "gold" from Granite Creek in the Similkameen district near Princeton and returned to B.C. However, Granite Creek had nearly petered out by the time he got there, and so he returned to his old stamping grounds at Lightning Creek. His last venture, several years before his death, was a tunnel on the side of Lightning Creek near Beaver Pass. He died in Vancouver.

Besides Jones and Evans, one other member of the Party is buried in Stanley Cemetery, but has no known resting place. He was Robert F. Pritchard, the company's blacksmith, who died in 1915.

LINDARD, *Yoachim Wilhelm. Sacred to the memory of, Native of Stege Denmark. Died June 9, 1873. Aged 38 years.* The *Sentinel* had this to say: "To his indomitable pluck, boundless faith, untiring energy and liberality, are the people of Lightning Creek indebted in no small degree for the success which has lately attended their efforts in opening of the mines of that district."

Lindhard operated one of the first "express" companies on the Harrison Lake-Lillooet trail in 1859, and came north to settle in Van Winkle in 1865. Shortly before his death he opened a meat market in Barkerville.

Capt. Evans read the burial service and "not one claim on Lightning Creek was worked. Every house and store was closed at an early hour, and remained so until night. Sorrow was depicted on every countenance."

PEEBLES, John. Born in Loghee, Scotland, Oct. 23, 1833. Died Sept. 2, 1889. At Rest.

SCHUETZY, E. In memory of. Aged 43 years. Died May 6, 1875.

STOTT, Abe. Born January 19, 1870. Rochdale, Lancashire, England. Died July 22, 1926. With Patrick McKenna, a former Chicago policeman, who lies buried in Cameronton Cemetery, Stott discovered gold at Eight-Mile Lake while on a fishing trip. Scientists and old timers maintained there could be no pay there. By trade Stott had been a window-dresser.

View of Stanley from cemetery, overlooking Costello Shaft

COSTELLO SHAFT: This shaft was sunk in the early 1870s at a cost of $37,493 and up to November 1875 had returned only $20,476. It proved to be the poorest mine on the creek and was abandoned the following year. In that year it is said to have paid expenses.

Stanley, 1899

STANLEY: Named in 1870 after Edward Henry Stanley (1826-1903), 15th Earl of Derby and Secretary of State for the Colonies at the time. His brother, Frederick Arthur Stanley, Baron Stanley of Preston, was Governor-General of Canada from 1888 to 1893 and left his name to Vancouver's beautiful Stanley Park.

Stanley's glory is in its past, and today only the shell of it remains. During Sam Montgomery's days (see Barkerville or Cameronton cemetery) it was a rip-roaring place with saloons, hotels, restaurants, etc. The last of these to operate was the Lightning Hotel, at the forks of the "old" and the "new" road to Barkerville. The old Cariboo Road approach to Barkerville carried on straight east from the Lightning Hotel, but is now practically impossible to pass over. Two miles east was the town of Van Winkle, which in 1863 had 25 business establishments, but by 1865 it was said to be "nearly deserted". It was still going, however, in the early 1890s, but now not a single vestige remains.

The present road to Barkerville from Stanley, up through the canyon and via Wells was built in 1885.

The stream which flows into Lightning Creek at Stanley is Chisholm Creek, a rich placer gold creek from the middle 1860s to its peak year of 1885 when $2,000 in gold was reported taken out.

Government reports estimate that the Stanley area has yielded placer gold estimated to have a value of $10,000,000 or more.

Stanley today

"The total placer gold production of the Stanley area," one report reads, "is not definitely known. In the Lightning Creek section the value of the officially recorded gold production since 1874 is $1,992,845. The total production since 1861 is conservatively estimated to be between $5,000,000 and $6,000,000 and may have been as much as about $12,000,000.... The bulk of the placer gold produced from Lightning Creek was mined along an 8,000 foot stretch extending downstream from the mouth of Van Winkle Creek almost to Stanley."

KETCH MINE: Coming up Chisholm Creek and through the narrow Devil's Canyon from Stanley it will be noticed that high in the hills can be seen what appears to be irrigation ditches, or the remains of them. These are the flumes taking water to the hydraulic operation conducted in 1921 onwards by W. H. Housser and John MacDougall at the Ketch Mine.

A climb up to the top of the tailings—a stiff one but not a long hike—will give a clear indication of how a hydraulic operation scours away all the overburden to get down to bedrock where the gold lies. This mine was not a great mine, but it did produce a nugget weighing over 16 ounces in 1937—the largest found in the area since the early days.

The mine is said to have been named on account of a saloon in the canyon whose owner hoped to "ketch" all the trade.